I0008034

MrBeast

and

The YouTuber Success Model

SOUTHERLAND | COPYRIGHT 2023

Introduction

In digital content creation, few stories resonate as profoundly as that of MrBeast, born Jimmy Donaldson. His meteoric rise to fame on YouTube is not just a tale of personal success but a narrative that has significantly influenced the YouTube community and the broader domain of digital content creation.

MrBeast embarked on his YouTube journey with modest beginnings. His early content, characterized by a mix of gaming, reaction videos, and challenges, gradually garnered attention. However, it was his unique blend of outrageous challenges, philanthropic gestures, and an innate understanding of the YouTube algorithm that catapulted him to stardom. His journey is a testament to the power of innovation, persistence, and an unwavering commitment to his vision.

MrBeast's rise to fame on YouTube is marked by his revolutionary approach to content. He redefined what it means to be a successful YouTuber, demonstrating that success on the platform can be achieved through creativity, strategic planning, and a keen sense of what resonates with the audience. His approach to content creation, community engagement, and philanthropy has influenced a generation of YouTubers, setting new standards and expectations for what can be achieved on the platform.

One of the most notable aspects of MrBeast's influence is his approach to philanthropy. By integrating charitable work into his content, he has not only contributed significantly to various causes but also inspired his viewers and fellow creators to engage in social good. His initiatives like #TeamTrees and #TeamSeas have shown how digital platforms can be leveraged for impactful philanthropic work.

The story of MrBeast is one of extraordinary success and influence in the realm of digital content creation. His journey from a regular YouTuber to an international icon encapsulates the essence of innovation, adaptability, and the power of digital media to create meaningful impact.

MrBeast Biography

Early Life

James Stephen Donaldson, better known as MrBeast, embarked on his journey into the world on May 7, 1998, in Wichita, Kansas. His early years were spent in Greenville, North Carolina, where the complexities of his upbringing began to shape his character and future. Born into a family where both parents had demanding careers, his childhood was marked by the presence of au pairs, who stepped in due to the combined pressures of his parents' work commitments and military service.

The year 2007 brought a significant shift in young James's life with the divorce of his parents. Such a pivotal event in a child's life often brings a mix of confusion and clarity, challenges and opportunities for growth. It was during these formative years that the seeds of resilience, adaptability, and creativity began to take root in him, qualities that would later become hallmarks of his success.

His academic journey saw him graduating from Greenville Christian Academy in 2016, a milestone that marked the end of his conventional schooling and the beginning of an unconventional path. Despite enrolling at East Carolina University, the pull towards a different destiny was too strong. YouTube, a platform bustling with creative potential and uncharted possibilities, beckoned him.

In a decisive move that would set the course for his extraordinary career, James Donaldson chose to drop out of college. This decision, bold and unconventional, was driven by a vision that extended beyond the traditional pathways of education and career. It was a leap of faith into a domain where he could harness his creativity, entrepreneurial spirit, and passion for making an impact.

This choice marked the beginning of an extraordinary journey, one that would see MrBeast not just as a participant in the digital world but as a trailblazer who would redefine the boundaries of content creation, philanthropy, and digital influence. His story, from the early years in Greenville to his rise as a YouTube sensation, is a testament to the power of pursuing one's passion against all odds, embracing the risks, and boldly stepping into the unknown.

MrBeast created his YouTube channel when he was just 13 years old, using the username "MrBeast6000." Initially, his content was quite different from what he is known for today. He began his YouTube journey by experimenting with various video formats and content ideas.

In his early years on YouTube, MrBeast primarily focused on creating gaming videos. He played and recorded gameplay from a variety of popular video games. These videos were aimed at the gaming community, where viewers often watch gameplay, seek tips, or enjoy entertainment related to their favorite games.

One of the unique content types MrBeast explored during this period was creating videos where he estimated the wealth of popular YouTubers. These videos often garnered attention and were viewed by fans of the creators he analyzed. These estimations were based on publicly available information, and they added an analytical and commentary aspect to his channel.

Similar to many content creators during that time, MrBeast occasionally delved into YouTube drama and controversies. He offered his insights and commentary on various incidents and conflicts within the YouTube community. This type of content allowed him to engage with trending topics and share his opinions.

Rise to Fame (2017–2020)

MrBeast's rise to fame from 2017 to 2020 marked a pivotal period in his YouTube career, during which he gained widespread recognition for his unique content and commitment to pushing the boundaries of what was possible on the platform. This period saw him achieve remarkable success and cement his position as one of the most prominent content creators on YouTube.

MrBeast's breakthrough came with the creation of the "Worst Intros on YouTube" series. In these videos, he humorously critiqued and roasted various YouTube channels' introductions, providing humorous commentary and sarcastic remarks. The series struck a chord with viewers and quickly gained popularity, attracting a significant audience interested in internet culture and YouTube drama.

What set MrBeast apart during this period was his willingness to experiment with bold and unconventional content. He was known for taking risks and coming up with ideas that stood out in the crowded YouTube landscape. His videos often featured eye-catching challenges, grand-scale giveaways, and philanthropic stunts.

A significant decision that marked his rise to fame was MrBeast's choice to drop out of college and commit to YouTube full-time. He made this decision as his channel gained momentum and his audience continued to grow. This bold move demonstrated his dedication to pursuing his passion and creating content that resonated with viewers.

During this period, MrBeast brought his childhood friends into the fold, hiring them to collaborate on his channel. These close-knit relationships added an authentic and relatable dimension to his content. His friends became integral to his videos, participating in challenges, and contributing to the camaraderie that viewers found engaging.

MrBeast's content began to evolve into a mix of entertaining challenges and philanthropic acts. He would create videos where he attempted audacious feats, such as counting to a million or watching a single video for 24 hours. These challenges often had significant monetary prizes attached, showcasing his willingness to give back to his audience in unique ways.

MrBeast's commitment to philanthropy became increasingly evident during this period. He started organizing charitable events and fundraisers, using his platform to raise funds for various causes. For example, he hosted events like "Last To Leave" challenges, where the last participant standing would win a substantial cash prize. He also donated substantial amounts to charities and community organizations, amplifying his impact beyond YouTube.

As a result of his innovative content and philanthropic efforts, MrBeast's channel experienced explosive growth during this period. He gained millions of subscribers and became one of the most talked-about creators on the platform. His work was widely recognized, earning him accolades and invitations to collaborate with other prominent YouTubers.

MrBeast's rise to fame from 2017 to 2020 was characterized by his daring content experiments, his dedication to philanthropy, and his decision to commit to YouTube full-time. His willingness to push the boundaries of traditional content creation, combined with his commitment to making a positive impact, helped him secure his place as a dominant force on YouTube and a respected figure in the online community.

Success and Accomplishments

MrBeast, whose real name is Jimmy Donaldson, has achieved remarkable success in the world of content creation and philanthropy. His accomplishments are a testament to his innovative approach, commitment to making a positive impact, and his ability to connect with a massive global audience. Here's a detailed look at some of his notable achievements:

MrBeast is the creator of multiple YouTube channels, each catering to different aspects of his content. While his main channel, "MrBeast," features a wide range of videos, he has also launched specialized channels like "MrBeast Gaming," where he explores the gaming world, and "Beast Philanthropy," which documents his charitable endeavors. This multi-channel approach allows him to diversify his content and engage with various audiences.

As part of his entrepreneurial ventures, MrBeast launched "MrBeast Burger," a virtual restaurant chain that operates through delivery apps. It offers a variety of burgers, fries, and other menu items. This move into the food industry showcases his innovative thinking beyond traditional YouTube content. Additionally, MrBeast has been involved in the creation of "Feastables," which combines cooking and gaming content on his gaming channel.

MrBeast's commitment to philanthropy is exemplified by his involvement in co-creating two groundbreaking fundraisers: "Team Trees" and "Team Seas."

Team Trees: In collaboration with the Arbor Day Foundation, MrBeast initiated "Team Trees" with the goal of planting 20 million trees worldwide by the end of 2019. This environmental campaign successfully reached its target, raising millions of dollars for tree planting efforts.

Team Seas: Following the success of "Team Trees," MrBeast and his team, along with other creators and organizations, launched "Team Seas" with the aim of removing 30 million pounds of plastic waste from the ocean. This ambitious project demonstrates his dedication to environmental causes.

MrBeast's contributions to YouTube and philanthropy have not gone unnoticed, and he has received several awards and accolades:

Streamy Awards' Creator of the Year: He has won the Streamy Awards' prestigious Creator of the Year title, highlighting his impact on the YouTube platform and the broader online community.

Nickelodeon Kids' Choice Awards' Favorite Male Creator: MrBeast has been recognized by younger viewers through the Nickelodeon Kids' Choice Awards, earning the title of Favorite Male Creator.

Variety's Power of Young Hollywood List: He has been featured on Variety's Power of Young Hollywood list, which showcases influential young talent in the entertainment industry.

Other Honors: MrBeast's philanthropic efforts have earned him recognition from various organizations and publications, further solidifying his position as a prominent online figure.

MrBeast's achievements extend far beyond his YouTube success. He has expanded his influence into entrepreneurial ventures, philanthropy, and environmental causes, while also earning awards and recognition for his contributions to the online and entertainment industries. His ability to combine innovative content creation with a genuine desire to make a positive impact has made him a standout figure in the digital realm.

Family Bonds: The Foundation of His Journey

Jimmy Donaldson, known as MrBeast, has frequently emphasized the importance of family in his life and career.

His family, particularly his mother, has played a significant role in his journey, both personally and professionally. MrBeast's close relationship with his family has been a grounding force, providing emotional support and stability amidst his rapid rise to fame.

A notably endearing aspect of MrBeast's videos is his relationship with his mother. She has appeared in several of his videos, participating in challenges and charity events. These appearances not only offer a glimpse into MrBeast's personal life but also highlight a supportive and loving family dynamic. The presence of his mother in his content brings a relatable and heartwarming element, resonating with viewers who value family connections.

This strong family bond has undoubtedly influenced MrBeast's approach to content creation and his philanthropic efforts. The values instilled in him by his family, such as kindness, generosity, and a sense of responsibility towards others, are evident in his work. His family's influence has helped shape his public persona, making him a relatable and admired figure among his audience.

Personal Health Journey

MrBeast has been candid about his personal struggle with Crohn's disease, a chronic inflammatory bowel condition that he has been managing since his teenage years. Crohn's disease, characterized by symptoms like abdominal pain, severe diarrhea, fatigue, and weight loss, poses significant physical and emotional challenges.

By openly discussing his battle with Crohn's disease, MrBeast has played a crucial role in raising awareness about this condition. His honesty about the struggles associated with managing a chronic illness has sparked conversations around health issues often not discussed publicly. His willingness to share his experiences provides comfort and support to others dealing with similar health challenges.

MrBeast's journey with Crohn's disease has added a layer of depth to his public image. It demonstrates his resilience and determination to succeed despite personal health challenges. His story is an inspiration to many, showing that it is possible to overcome adversity and achieve significant accomplishments.

Relationships

MrBeast has been involved in a few public relationships. We will not go into great detail here, but here is an overview of key relationships.

Maddy Spidell

Maddy Spidell, like MrBeast, is a content creator on YouTube. She gained recognition for her lifestyle and vlogging content, which often featured aspects of her daily life, travel adventures, and personal experiences. Her videos resonated with a broad audience interested in her relatable and engaging content.

Maddy Spidell's prominence in the online world significantly increased when she entered into a romantic relationship with MrBeast. Their relationship became highly public, and they frequently featured each other in their respective social media posts and YouTube videos. This transparency allowed fans and viewers to witness their interactions and shared moments, both in their personal lives and in collaborative content.

The relationship between Maddy Spidell and MrBeast was generally well-received by their fans and followers. Their genuine chemistry and affection for each other resonated with viewers, and many found their interactions heartwarming and relatable. This public display of affection added a personal touch to their content, which helped connect them even more strongly with their audience.

It's important to acknowledge that relationships, especially those in the public eye, can evolve and change over time. Individuals in the public eye often face additional pressures and scrutiny. While Maddy Spidell and MrBeast shared a close bond during their time together, they eventually went their separate ways.

Thea Booysen

Thea Booysen is a notable figure in the world of YouTube and social media, primarily recognized for her association with MrBeast (Jimmy Donaldson). As of my last knowledge update in January 2022, she was reported to be in a relationship with MrBeast, and her involvement in his content had garnered significant attention from fans and the online community.

Thea Booysen has her own presence on social media, particularly on Instagram, where she shares aspects of her life, travel experiences, and personal interests. While she may not have a dedicated YouTube channel of her own, her Instagram and presence in MrBeast's content have contributed to her visibility in the online world.

Thea Booysen has been actively involved in MrBeast's YouTube videos and social media content. She often makes appearances alongside MrBeast in his videos, participating in various challenges, philanthropic endeavors, and charitable acts. Her participation adds an element of companionship and camaraderie to MrBeast's content, which resonates with his audience.

Thea Booysen's connection with MrBeast has been a subject of interest among fans. They are often seen together in public outings, on social media, and during MrBeast's content creation. Their relationship appears to be a positive and supportive aspect of their lives, as reflected in their interactions on camera.

Thea Booysen's presence has contributed to the relatability and human aspect of MrBeast's content. Her involvement showcases the personal side of MrBeast, which resonates with viewers who appreciate the genuine and authentic interactions between the two. This has allowed fans to connect with MrBeast on a deeper level.

Philanthropic Journey

MrBeast's philanthropic journey began with the realization of the potential of his YouTube platform to make a positive impact on the world. He decided to use his growing popularity to give back to those in need, marking the inception of his role as an online philanthropist. One of the ways he did this was by incorporating charity into his YouTube content.

In addition to his main YouTube channel, MrBeast created a dedicated channel called "Beast Philanthropy." This channel focuses specifically on documenting his various charitable endeavors, fundraising events, and acts of kindness. Through Beast Philanthropy, viewers can witness the impact of his donations and charity work in a transparent and detailed manner.

MrBeast is renowned for his extravagant and large-scale acts of charity. He has undertaken numerous jaw-dropping initiatives, such as giving away thousands of dollars to random strangers, donating to food banks, covering bills for restaurant patrons, and even purchasing and renovating houses for those in need. His willingness to go to great lengths to help others has garnered immense respect from his audience.

One of MrBeast's most notable philanthropic projects is the "Team Trees" initiative. In collaboration with other prominent YouTubers and the Arbor Day Foundation, MrBeast spearheaded a campaign to plant 20 million trees by raising funds from viewers. The campaign was a massive success, reaching its goal and showcasing the collective power of the online community to make a positive environmental impact.

MrBeast has also made substantial donations to Feeding America, a non-profit organization dedicated to addressing hunger in the United States. His contributions have helped provide millions of meals to those facing food insecurity, especially during challenging times such as the COVID-19 pandemic.

During the COVID-19 pandemic, MrBeast launched initiatives to support small businesses that were struggling due to lockdowns and restrictions. He would order large quantities of food from local restaurants, tip generously, and encourage his audience to do the same, thereby aiding these businesses during difficult times.

Perhaps one of MrBeast's most significant impacts is his ability to inspire others to give back. His philanthropic acts often challenge viewers to consider the positive changes they can make in their communities. Many individuals and content creators have been inspired to launch their charitable initiatives as a result of his example.

MrBeast's philanthropy extends beyond his YouTube channel, becoming a significant part of his identity and a source of inspiration for millions of viewers. His commitment to making the world a better place through acts of kindness, generosity, and charity has solidified his status as a leading figure in online philanthropy, and his Beast Philanthropy channel continues to showcase his dedication to giving back to the community.

#TeamTrees - A Record-Breaking Environmental Initiative

MrBeast, known for his philanthropic ventures, made a significant impact through various campaigns, most notably the #TeamTrees initiative. Launched in October 2019, #TeamTrees became the most successful crowdfunding effort in YouTube's history and one of the fastest-growing environmental fundraisers to date.

The campaign began as a challenge to MrBeast (Jimmy Donaldson) to plant 20 million trees in commemoration of reaching 20 million subscribers on his YouTube channel. Collaborating with fellow YouTuber and former NASA scientist Mark Rober, and partnering with the Arbor Day Foundation, they set out to achieve this ambitious goal.

The fundraising goal of $20 million was achieved in only 56 days, driven by the enthusiasm and contributions from the online community, including half a million individual donations in just two months. Notable contributions came from industry tech leaders like Elon Musk, Salesforce CEO Marc Benioff, YouTube CEO Susan Wojcicki, and Shopify CEO Tobi Lütke, each donating significant amounts to the cause.

As of June 5, 2021, #TeamTrees reached a donation milestone of $23 million, which will be used to plant 23 million trees. These trees are being planted across the globe in various forests on both public and private lands in areas of great need. The initiative remains on track to complete the planting of the original 20 million trees by the end of 2022, despite challenges posed by the COVID-19 pandemic.

The environmental impact of planting 20 million trees is significant, akin to taking 1.24 million cars off the road for a year. This demonstrates the positive effect on air quality, water filtration, and forest ecosystems.

#TeamTrees, with the ongoing support of the Arbor Day Foundation and its planting partners, has physically planted more than 8 million trees worldwide to date. The initiative continues to receive donations every single day, underscoring the sustained interest and support from the global community.

This philanthropic campaign is a prime example of how social media and influencer platforms can be leveraged to address critical societal issues and foster a sense of global community and environmental responsibility. MrBeast's commitment to making a positive impact on the world through initiatives like #TeamTrees showcases the incredible potential of online communities to drive change and create a better future for the planet.

Controversies

In 2018, MrBeast faced a series of accusations related to his YouTube channel and his treatment of employees. These accusations, which circulated online and among some members of the YouTube community, raised concerns about the authenticity of his content and how he managed his growing channel. MrBeast, who is known for his philanthropic stunts and attention-grabbing challenges, responded to these allegations by addressing them directly and providing his perspective.

One of the primary accusations against MrBeast in 2018 was that he was faking some of the content on his channel. Critics claimed that some of his videos, which often featured extravagant giveaways and expensive challenges, were staged or exaggerated for views and engagement. They argued that it was improbable for him to afford the extravagant prizes he offered, such as cars or large sums of money.

MrBeast responded to these allegations by explaining that while some aspects of his videos might be scripted for entertainment purposes, the core of his content was genuine. He maintained that the giveaways and challenges were real, and the prizes he offered were funded through sponsorships, brand deals, and his own investments. He acknowledged that the content might appear exaggerated at times but argued that it was essential to capture the audience's attention in a competitive YouTube landscape.

Another set of accusations in 2018 focused on MrBeast's treatment of his employees and associates. Some individuals claimed that he was exploiting his friends and colleagues by making them work long hours without fair compensation. There were allegations of a lack of transparency regarding the financial aspects of his channel and concerns that some individuals involved were not adequately compensated for their contributions.

In response to these accusations, MrBeast asserted that he valued his team and collaborators and that they were all compensated fairly. He explained that many of his friends and colleagues were genuinely passionate about the content they created and the mission of his channel. While the work could be intense and demanding, he maintained that everyone involved was there voluntarily and with full knowledge of the goals and expectations.

Following these accusations, MrBeast made efforts to increase transparency about the financial aspects of his channel. He started to share more details about how he funded his ambitious giveaways and charitable acts, including sponsorships and partnerships with brands. This transparency aimed to address concerns about the sustainability of his content and the sources of funding.

In the years since these accusations emerged, MrBeast's channel has continued to grow, and he has become one of the most prominent and influential YouTubers. He has maintained his commitment to philanthropy, frequently using his platform to give back to communities and support charitable causes.

Ventures and Collaborations

One cannot delve into MrBeast's collaborative ventures without mentioning some of the most prominent names in the YouTube sphere. Mark Rober, PewDiePie, Casey Neistat, and David Dobrik are just a few of the luminaries who have joined forces with MrBeast. These collaborations have not only expanded MrBeast's reach but have also brought diverse perspectives, styles, and fanbases into his orbit.

Collaborations on YouTube are not mere partnerships; they are an alchemical fusion of creativity, audience engagement, and shared goals. When MrBeast collaborates with fellow YouTubers, it's not just about creating content together; it's about creating moments, experiences, and narratives that resonate with millions.

Mark Rober, known for his scientific prowess and engaging educational content, has joined forces with MrBeast on multiple occasions. Together, they've tackled challenges that blend science, engineering, and entertainment. Whether it's launching a rocket-powered car or attempting to survive on a deserted island, their collaborations have captivated audiences and garnered millions of views. It's a testament to the magic that happens when two creators with distinct styles come together to push the boundaries of what's possible on YouTube.

PewDiePie, the reigning king of YouTube with a massive global following, is another key collaborator in MrBeast's roster. Their collaborations have not only generated astronomical view counts but have also showcased the camaraderie that exists among top YouTubers. From hosting the 'Minecraft Championship' event to engaging in friendly competitions, their collaborations have been a source of entertainment and connection for millions of viewers.

Casey Neistat, a trailblazer in the world of vlogging and storytelling, has also left his mark on MrBeast's content. Their collaboration on a 'Real Life Squid Game' video combined Neistat's cinematic storytelling prowess with MrBeast's penchant for grandeur challenges. The result was a captivating and emotionally charged video that resonated deeply with their combined audiences.

David Dobrik, known for his high-energy vlogs and viral pranks, has brought his signature style to the world of MrBeast. Their collaboration in a massive game of hide-and-seek turned a childhood pastime into an epic adventure. It's a testament to the versatility of MrBeast's content that he can seamlessly integrate his fellow YouTubers into his challenges, creating content that feels both authentic and engaging.

MrBeast's influence extends beyond YouTube content creation. He has ventured into the realm of tech startups and partnered with financial networks to support fellow creators. These endeavors showcase his entrepreneurial spirit and commitment to nurturing the YouTube ecosystem.

Investing in tech startups allows MrBeast to diversify his portfolio and support innovative companies in the tech industry. His financial acumen and business instincts have led him to explore opportunities beyond the confines of YouTube, positioning him as a multifaceted entrepreneur with a keen eye for promising ventures.

Partnering with financial networks for creator support is a testament to MrBeast's commitment to giving back to the YouTube community. By collaborating with established financial institutions, he empowers creators to navigate the complexities of financial management, investment, and wealth building. This initiative not only provides creators with valuable resources but also fosters a sense of financial literacy and responsibility within the YouTube ecosystem.

MrBeast's foray into business ventures and collaborations exemplifies the multifaceted nature of his influence in the digital realm. His collaborations with prominent YouTubers bring together diverse creative forces, resulting in content that resonates with millions. His dedicated team, including childhood friends and key personnel, serves as the backbone of his operation, ensuring the smooth execution of his ambitious projects. Moreover, his investments in tech startups and partnerships with financial networks underscore his commitment to fostering innovation and financial literacy within the YouTube community. Beyond YouTube content creation, MrBeast's ventures and collaborations serve as a testament to his entrepreneurial spirit and his dedication to leaving a lasting impact on the digital landscape.

Net Worth

MrBeast had amassed considerable wealth through his various endeavors, primarily centered around his YouTube channel and associated business ventures. It is estimated that his net worth is approximately $500 million. However, it's important to note that specific details about his net worth and assets can fluctuate and may not be publicly disclosed in full.

Here's a look at is revenue sources based on available information:

YouTube Revenue: MrBeast's primary source of income is his YouTube channel. With millions of subscribers and billions of views across his videos, he earns significant revenue from YouTube's Partner Program through advertisements placed in his videos. The exact earnings can vary greatly based on factors like video view count, engagement rates, and the types of advertisements shown, but it's estimated that top YouTubers can earn several million dollars annually from ad revenue alone.

Sponsorships and Brand Deals: A substantial portion of MrBeast's income also comes from sponsorships and brand deals. He has partnered with various companies, promoting products or services in his videos. These deals are often lucrative, with top influencers like MrBeast commanding high fees for sponsored content. The exact figures for these sponsorships are usually confidential, but they significantly boost his earnings.

Merchandise Sales: MrBeast has capitalized on his brand by selling merchandise, including apparel and other branded products. His merchandise sales contribute a considerable amount to his overall income. The success of such merchandise is often tied to the influencer's popularity and the loyalty of their fan base.

Business Ventures: Beyond YouTube, MrBeast has diversified into several business ventures. One notable example is MrBeast Burger, a virtual restaurant brand that operates on a delivery-only model. He also launched Feastables, a snack food brand. These ventures not only represent direct sources of income but also enhance his overall brand value.

Investments and Collaborations: MrBeast has also been involved in various investments and collaborations. This includes investing in tech startups and collaborating with other content creators and businesses. These investments and partnerships potentially contribute to his wealth, though specifics about returns and earnings from these endeavors are not typically disclosed.

Philanthropic Channel: MrBeast also runs a philanthropic channel, Beast Philanthropy, where he documents his charitable activities. While this channel might not directly contribute to his wealth, it's a significant part of his brand identity, which indirectly supports his other revenue-generating activities.

Real Estate and Assets: Details about MrBeast's personal assets, such as real estate holdings, are not widely publicized. Influencers often invest in property and other assets as part of their wealth management strategy, but specific information about such investments is usually private.

While it's challenging to pinpoint an exact figure for MrBeast's net worth without access to his personal financial details, it's clear that his diverse income streams from YouTube, sponsorships, merchandise, business ventures, and investments have contributed to a substantial accumulation of wealth. His success story is a testament to the potential of digital platforms like YouTube for content monetization and brand building.

The Business

The Need for a Team

In the early stages of his YouTube career, MrBeast, like many content creators, began as a one-man show. His initial videos, characterized by their unique blend of humor, audacity, and generosity, quickly garnered a substantial following. However, as his ambitions scaled, so did the complexity and scope of his projects. Recognizing the limitations of working solo and the multifaceted nature of his expanding brand, MrBeast began to assemble a team of skilled individuals who could bring diverse perspectives and expertise to the table.

The content creators in his team are responsible for brainstorming and executing the unique video ideas that MrBeast is known for. Their creative inputs are critical in maintaining the high engagement levels of his videos. Marketers, on the other hand, ensure that his content reaches the widest possible audience. They strategize on distribution channels, social media promotions, and audience engagement techniques that amplify his reach.

Strategists in his team play a vital role in navigating the ever-changing landscape of digital content and business. They help in identifying new opportunities for growth, whether in terms of content, partnerships, or business expansions. Their strategic insights are crucial for making informed decisions that align with MrBeast's brand vision and goals.

In addition to his core team, MrBeast also collaborates with external partners and experts when necessary. These collaborations bring additional expertise and resources, further enhancing the quality and impact of his work.

The Backbone

Behind every successful YouTuber stands a dedicated team that keeps the wheels of creativity turning. MrBeast's journey is no exception, and his team has played a pivotal role in his rise to digital stardom.

Chris Tyson, a childhood friend of MrBeast, has been an integral part of the team. As the Chief Operating Officer, Tyson oversees the day-to-day operations of MrBeast's ventures, ensuring that everything runs smoothly. His unwavering dedication and business acumen have been instrumental in scaling MrBeast's philanthropic endeavors.

Chandler Hallow, often a key figure in MrBeast's videos, has been a close friend and collaborator. Known for his calm demeanor and willingness to undertake daring challenges, Chandler has become a fan favorite. His involvement in MrBeast's content adds a layer of authenticity and relatability that resonates with viewers.

Garrett Ronalds, another essential member of the team, has been responsible for managing MrBeast's social media presence. In the world of digital content, effective social media engagement is paramount, and Garrett's role in maintaining MrBeast's online persona is invaluable.

Jake Franklin, who manages partnerships and collaborations, has been the linchpin in MrBeast's expansive network of influencers and brands. His ability to forge strategic alliances has opened doors to new opportunities and expanded MrBeast's reach.

The composition of MrBeast's team is a testament to his understanding of the various facets of successful content creation and business management. This team comprises individuals with a range of skills, including but not limited to video production, graphic design, marketing, business strategy, and project management. Each member plays a critical role in the ideation, development, execution, and promotion of content, ensuring that every video meets the high standards MrBeast's audience has come to expect.

Marketers and Strategists

The marketing team's contribution to MrBeast's brand is invaluable. In an online world where viewer attention is fleeting, the ability to effectively promote content and engage with the audience is crucial. MrBeast's marketing team employs a variety of strategies to ensure maximum visibility and impact of each video. This includes optimizing content for different social media platforms, developing promotional campaigns, and leveraging analytics to understand audience preferences and behaviors. Their efforts ensure that MrBeast's content reaches a wide audience, driving both viewership and revenue.

The strategists in MrBeast's team are responsible for long-term planning and business development. They identify new opportunities for growth, whether through emerging social media platforms, potential brand partnerships, or innovative content formats. They also play a vital role in managing and diversifying MrBeast's revenue streams, which include YouTube ad revenue, brand sponsorships, merchandise sales, and philanthropic ventures.

Investment in Production Resources

Beyond human capital, MrBeast's investment in high-quality production resources has been pivotal in his success. He has consistently allocated a significant portion of his revenue towards upgrading equipment, securing filming locations, and enhancing production quality. This commitment to high production values is evident in the cinematic quality of his videos, which often resemble mini-movies rather than traditional YouTube content.

The journey of building and sustaining a successful content creation team is fraught with challenges.

MrBeast's team has navigated issues such as content burnout, maintaining consistency in quality, and adapting to the ever-changing algorithms of social media platforms. The team's ability to overcome these challenges is a testament to their collective skills, adaptability, and commitment to the MrBeast brand.

Content Evolution

The journey of MrBeast, born Jimmy Donaldson, in the realm of digital content creation is a fascinating study of evolution, innovation, and adaptation. His content, initially rooted in the gaming and reaction video genres, has undergone significant transformations, culminating in a unique brand that blends entertainment, philanthropy, and extraordinary challenges. This detailed analysis focuses on the evolution of MrBeast's content, the key turning points in his career, and the viral videos that have come to define his legacy.

MrBeast's early forays into YouTube were characterized by gaming videos, estimating the wealth of other YouTubers, and various project-based challenges. These initial videos, while showcasing his creativity and enthusiasm, did not immediately catapult him to YouTube stardom. However, they laid the foundation for his understanding of the platform and his audience.

A significant turning point in MrBeast's content creation journey was his shift towards challenge and stunt videos.

This transition marked a departure from conventional YouTube content, offering viewers something unique and captivating. His challenges, often involving large sums of money, endurance tests, and complex logistics, started to gain viral traction, setting the stage for his rapid rise in popularity.

Perhaps the most defining aspect of MrBeast's evolution as a content creator is the integration of philanthropic activities into his videos. He began incorporating acts of generosity and charity into his content, creating a new genre of philanthropic entertainment on YouTube. This move not only amplified his popularity but also set a new precedent for how influencers could leverage their platforms for social good.

As his channel grew, so did the scale and complexity of his videos. MrBeast started producing content that resembled large-scale productions, involving intricate setups, numerous participants, and significant financial investments. These videos, often resembling game shows or reality TV challenges, have become a hallmark of his brand.

Several of MrBeast's videos have achieved viral status, garnering millions of views and solidifying his position as a top-tier content creator. Videos such as "I Spent 50 Hours Buried Alive," "I Put 100 Million Orbeez In My Friend's Backyard," and his recreation of the "Squid Game" series, have transcended the usual confines of

YouTube content, drawing attention from a global audience.

Throughout his career, MrBeast has demonstrated an impressive ability to adapt to changes in YouTube's algorithm, platform policies, and audience preferences. His content evolution is not just a reflection of his creative growth but also his strategic thinking in aligning his content with the dynamic digital landscape.

Art of Engagement

MrBeast, a luminary in this domain, has not only mastered the art of content creation but also the nuanced art of engaging his audience. His strategies in viewer engagement stand as a testament to his deep understanding of audience psychology and platform mechanics. This detailed analysis delves into the strategies MrBeast employs to engage viewers and his unique approach to content creation and audience interaction.

At the heart of MrBeast's engagement strategy lies his ability to craft compelling narratives. His videos are more than just a sequence of events; they tell stories that evoke emotions, suspense, and curiosity. By structuring his content around narratives that resonate with viewers, he transforms passive viewing into an interactive experience. This storytelling approach not only retains the audience's attention but also encourages them to invest emotionally in the content.

MrBeast's challenges are uniquely interactive and immersive, often involving his audience directly or indirectly. Whether it's through participation challenges, viewer-driven content, or providing opportunities for fans to engage in real-time, his approach ensures that viewers are not mere spectators but active participants in the narrative.

A significant aspect of MrBeast's content is the element of surprise and his generous giveaways. By incorporating unexpected turns and substantial rewards, he creates a sense of anticipation and excitement in his videos. This strategy not only enhances viewer engagement but also fosters a positive association with his brand, encouraging repeated viewership.

Understanding the importance of shareability in the digital age, MrBeast creates content that viewers are compelled to share. His videos often feature elements that are relatable, astonishing, or emotionally stirring, making them ideal for sharing on social media platforms. This approach extends his reach beyond his subscriber base, drawing in a broader audience.

MrBeast extends his engagement strategies beyond YouTube, utilizing social media platforms to build a community around his brand. He interacts with his audience through various social media channels, keeping them updated, seeking their opinions, and involving them in his content creation process. This multi-platform engagement strengthens his relationship with viewers, making them feel like a part of his journey.

Consistent interaction with his audience and incorporating their feedback into his content creation is a hallmark of MrBeast's strategy. He actively engages with comments, responds to feedback, and adjusts his content based on audience preferences. This responsive approach not only enhances viewer satisfaction but also fosters a sense of community and loyalty.

Philanthropy Impact on Branding

The dynamics of viewer engagement in philanthropic content are complex but hold the potential to foster a deep sense of trust and authenticity, provided that a delicate balance between entertainment and social responsibility is maintained.

Philanthropic content often triggers a unique form of viewer engagement. When viewers witness acts of kindness, charity, or social impact, they are emotionally moved and inspired to engage more deeply with the content. In MrBeast's case, viewers are not just passive observers; they become active participants in the charitable endeavors. They feel a sense of ownership in the philanthropic mission, often contributing through donations, sharing the content, or participating in related challenges.

Philanthropic content evokes powerful emotions, such as empathy, gratitude, and hope. MrBeast's videos, showcasing generous giveaways and support to those in need, strike an emotional chord with viewers. This emotional connection transcends the entertainment aspect of the content, making it more meaningful and memorable. Viewers appreciate content creators who use their platforms for positive change, and this appreciation fosters trust.

Maintaining a balance between entertainment and social responsibility is crucial in philanthropic content. While the core purpose is to make a positive impact, it's equally important to create content that is engaging and enjoyable to watch. MrBeast excels in this regard by infusing humor, suspense, and creativity into his philanthropic endeavors. This balance ensures that viewers are not only inspired by the charitable acts but also entertained throughout the video.

Philanthropic content reinforces viewer trust in several ways. First, it demonstrates the authenticity of the content creator's intentions. When viewers see tangible acts of kindness and social impact, they believe that the creator genuinely cares about making a difference. Second, transparency plays a vital role. MrBeast and his team provide detailed information about the funds raised, the charities supported, and the outcomes achieved, ensuring that viewers have full visibility into the philanthropic process. This transparency builds trust.

MrBeast's brand authenticity is deeply intertwined with his philanthropic efforts. By consistently incorporating charity into his content, he has created a brand that is synonymous with generosity and social responsibility. Viewers trust his brand because they have seen him consistently deliver on his promises to help others. His authenticity is further reinforced through candid moments, where he showcases the challenges and setbacks faced during charitable acts, making him relatable and genuine.

Philanthropic content has the potential to foster a unique and emotionally charged form of viewer engagement. When the delicate balance between entertainment and social responsibility is maintained, this content reinforces viewer trust and enhances brand authenticity. MrBeast's success in this domain is a testament to how philanthropy can be seamlessly integrated into digital content, forging a deeper connection with the audience and inspiring positive change.

Diversified Business Strategy

MrBeast's journey to success on YouTube was marked not only by his content creation prowess but also by his astute understanding of the need for a diversified business model. Recognizing that relying solely on ad revenue was limiting, he set out to expand his income streams. Beyond YouTube ads, MrBeast ventured into brand partnerships, merchandise sales, and even the food industry with his unique venture, MrBeast Burger. This diversification of income not only fortified his financial stability but also extended his brand presence across multiple sectors, creating a resilient and multifaceted business model. It's a testament to his entrepreneurial spirit and strategic thinking.

Central to MrBeast's business strategy is his approach to brand partnerships and collaborations. He's highly selective in choosing brands that align with his image and resonate with his audience. This careful curation ensures that his partnerships are not only lucrative but also authentic and engaging. These collaborations come in various forms, from small-scale promotional deals to substantial joint ventures, all of which have played a pivotal role in expanding his brand's reach and reinforcing its position in the market. MrBeast's ability to form meaningful and mutually beneficial brand relationships sets him apart as a shrewd businessman.

A strong presence on social media and the adept use of technology are essential for business growth. MrBeast recognizes the significance of these aspects in maintaining and expanding his influence. He leverages social media platforms strategically to promote his content, connect with his audience, and keep them engaged. Furthermore, his commitment to embracing the latest technology in content production and distribution keeps him at the forefront of innovation in a rapidly evolving digital environment. This ability to adapt and stay technologically relevant underscores his forward-thinking approach to business.

Behind MrBeast's meteoric rise is a robust team and infrastructure that supports the multifaceted aspects of his enterprise. He has assembled a team of professionals, including content creators, business managers, marketing experts, and other specialists who complement his skills and vision. This cohesive and talented team is essential for managing the complexities of a dynamic and expanding business. It's a testament to his leadership and organizational acumen, demonstrating that behind every successful content creator is a well-oiled team.

As MrBeast's brand grew, so did the challenges of scaling his business. This chapter examines the hurdles encountered during the expansion of his enterprise and the strategies employed to overcome them. Challenges include managing increased operational complexities, sustaining growth momentum, and adapting to the ever-changing market dynamics. Through a combination of innovation, resilience, and strategic planning, MrBeast has triumphed over these challenges, solidifying his position as a leading figure in the digital content creation and business world.

Collaborative Dynamics

At the heart of MrBeast's remarkable success in content creation lies the principle of collaboration. This section delves into the intricate dynamics of teamwork that drive the conception and realization of his ambitious video projects. For MrBeast and his team, collaboration is not just about dividing tasks; it's about sharing a vision and leveraging collective creativity to create content that captivates millions.

The journey of crafting a MrBeast video often commences with brainstorming sessions. In these gatherings, team members come together to pitch ideas, build upon each other's suggestions, and collectively select concepts that resonate with their brand and align with audience interests. These brainstorming sessions are characterized by a democratic spirit, where every team member is encouraged to contribute and refine ideas. This inclusive approach ensures a diverse range of perspectives and nurtures a creative environment where innovative concepts can flourish.

Once an idea is chosen, the team dives into the development phase. Here, each member's role becomes more defined. For example, Chris Tyson may focus on injecting entertainment value, Chandler Hallow brings his unique humor, Garrett Ronalds manages logistics, and Jake Franklin contributes to the creative storyline. While these roles may appear distinct, they are deeply interconnected, ensuring that every aspect of the video is meticulously crafted and seamlessly cohesive.

The strength of MrBeast's team lies in its ability to seamlessly integrate diverse skill sets. From technical expertise in filming and editing to creative writing and project management, each team member's skills play a pivotal role in transforming an idea into a viral video. This section sheds light on specific instances where the unique abilities of team members have elevated the content, adding depth and dimension to their videos.

The true test of the collaborative spirit comes during the execution phase. On the ground, challenges are bound to arise, be it logistical hurdles, technical glitches, or last-minute alterations. It is during these moments that the team's ability to work harmoniously, adapt swiftly, and solve problems on the fly shines through. This part of the chapter offers insights into real-life examples of how the team has navigated challenges during shoots, illustrating their adaptability and exemplary teamwork.

A hallmark of MrBeast's collaborative approach is the unwavering value placed on each team member's input. Suggestions and feedback are not only welcomed but are integral to the decision-making process. This inclusive culture fosters a sense of ownership and commitment among team members, propelling them to invest wholeheartedly in the success of each project.

The collaborative dynamics within MrBeast's team serve as the bedrock for the creation of content that resonates with millions. This section demonstrates how effective collaboration, which amalgamates diverse talents and perspectives, underpins the production of some of the most viral content on YouTube. It stands as a testament to the power of teamwork in the creative process and serves as a model for aspiring content creators looking to make their mark in the digital realm.

Power of Creative Marketing

One of MrBeast's hallmarks as a content creator and entrepreneur is his innovative approach to marketing. This section delves into the creative methods he employs to market his content, highlighting his use of interactive challenges that not only engage viewers but also encourage participation and sharing, effectively amplifying the reach of his content.

At the heart of MrBeast's marketing strategy are interactive challenges that serve as engaging hooks for his audience. These challenges range from daring stunts to thought-provoking social experiments. By introducing these challenges early in his videos, he captures viewers' attention and keeps them hooked throughout the content.

What sets MrBeast apart is his ability to transform passive viewers into active participants. He often integrates challenges that invite viewers to take action, whether it's solving riddles, guessing outcomes, or participating in online contests. This level of engagement not only makes viewers feel involved but also encourages them to stay tuned until the challenge's conclusion.

Many of MrBeast's challenges are designed to go viral. They are inherently shareable because they tap into universal themes, emotions, or curiosities. When viewers witness something extraordinary or entertaining, they are more likely to share it with their friends and family. This word-of-mouth promotion can lead to content going viral, rapidly expanding its reach.

MrBeast's challenges often evoke strong emotions in viewers. Whether it's the joy of witnessing someone receive a life-changing gift or the suspense of a high-stakes competition, his content strikes an emotional chord. These emotional responses drive viewers to share the content, wanting to spread the feelings they experienced.

MrBeast effectively uses social media platforms, including Twitter, Instagram, and TikTok, to promote his challenges and content. He provides teasers, behind-the-scenes glimpses, and countdowns to build anticipation among his followers. This cross-platform promotion ensures that his content reaches a broader audience beyond YouTube.

Collaborations are a significant part of MrBeast's marketing arsenal. By involving other YouTubers and social media influencers in his challenges, he taps into their existing fanbases. This not only introduces his content to new viewers but also encourages cross-promotion, as collaborating creators share the videos with their own audiences.

MrBeast is a master of building anticipation. He often teases upcoming challenges, hinting at their scale or impact. Viewers eagerly await these challenges, and the excitement generated in the lead-up ensures that when the video is finally released, it garners immediate attention and engagement.

MrBeast frequently rewards viewer engagement. For instance, he might offer cash prizes or giveaways to those who participate actively in challenges or engage with his content through likes, comments, or shares. These incentives not only boost engagement but also foster a sense of community among his viewers.

Building a Community Around the Brand

MrBeast's success is not solely attributed to creating engaging content but also to building a dedicated community around his brand. This section explores how he actively nurtures this sense of community among his followers, which in turn becomes a potent marketing tool.

One of the key ways MrBeast fosters a sense of community is through interactive engagement. He goes beyond the role of a content creator and actively interacts with his audience. This includes responding to comments on his videos, hosting live Q&A sessions, and engaging with fans on social media platforms like Twitter, Instagram, and TikTok.

By directly communicating with his audience, MrBeast creates a more personal and relatable connection. Viewers feel heard and valued, strengthening their loyalty to his brand. This open dialogue also provides insights into viewer preferences and feedback, which he can incorporate into future content.

MrBeast often involves his audience in challenges and contests. These can range from trivia quizzes during live streams to participatory challenges where viewers can win prizes or even be featured in his videos. These interactive events not only entertain but also create a sense of belonging and excitement among his followers.

Participation in these challenges becomes a badge of honor for his fans. It reinforces their connection to the MrBeast community and motivates them to engage more deeply with his content. It's a powerful way to transform passive viewers into active participants and promoters.

Transparency and authenticity are foundational elements of MrBeast's brand. He shares behind-the-scenes glimpses of his content creation process, showcases the impact of his philanthropic efforts, and provides updates on ongoing projects. This transparency builds trust and credibility with his audience.

MrBeast's willingness to admit mistakes and learn from them further humanizes him in the eyes of his viewers. This authenticity is a stark contrast to the polished personas of some content creators and strengthens the emotional connection with his audience.

The sense of community MrBeast has cultivated is a powerful marketing tool. His loyal fanbase is not only more likely to consume his content but also to promote it organically. They share videos, discuss his content in online forums, and introduce friends and family to his channel.

This word-of-mouth marketing, driven by a passionate and engaged community, significantly expands his content's reach. It's a testament to the value of building a strong and connected audience, transcending mere viewership to create a devoted fanbase that actively contributes to his brand's growth.

Collaborations and Cross-Promotion

MrBeast's strategic collaborations with a diverse range of YouTubers and social media personalities have played a pivotal role in his rise to success. This chapter delves into how these collaborations go beyond content creation and include joint promotional efforts, benefiting all parties involved.

One of the key advantages of collaborating with other content creators is the ability to tap into their existing audiences. MrBeast strategically chooses collaborators whose content aligns with his and who have substantial followings. This not only introduces his content to new viewers but also creates a sense of credibility and endorsement within the collaborators' fanbase.

These collaborations often involve guest appearances, challenges, or special events that offer something unique to both sets of viewers. For example, teaming up with another popular creator for a challenge video can create anticipation and excitement among both fanbases, driving higher engagement and views.

MrBeast's collaborations are intentionally diverse, encompassing creators from various niches and backgrounds. This diversity ensures that his content reaches a wide spectrum of viewers, enhancing his brand's visibility and appeal.

For instance, a collaboration with a tech-focused YouTuber might introduce his content to tech enthusiasts, while partnering with a lifestyle vlogger could attract a different demographic. This breadth of collaborations allows MrBeast to remain relevant to a broad audience.

Collaborations with fellow YouTubers and social media personalities often extend beyond the video itself. MrBeast and his collaborators engage in joint promotional efforts that amplify the reach of their content. This can include co-promoting videos on each other's channels, cross-promoting on social media platforms, and even running joint giveaways or contests.

These promotional efforts leverage the combined reach of both creators, resulting in increased visibility and engagement. It's a mutually beneficial strategy where both parties stand to gain from the cross-promotion.

While many collaborations are one-off events, MrBeast also nurtures long-term relationships with fellow creators. This fosters an ongoing synergy that benefits both sides. Over time, these relationships can lead to recurring collaborations and a sense of camaraderie that adds authenticity to the content.

Merchandising Advantage

Merchandising plays a significant role in MrBeast's marketing strategy, serving as a powerful tool to reinforce brand recognition and loyalty. This section explores how MrBeast effectively integrates merchandising into his overall approach, creating a win-win scenario for both his brand and his dedicated fanbase.

One of the primary benefits of merchandising for content creators like MrBeast is the diversification of revenue streams. Relying solely on ad revenue can be limiting, and merchandising provides an additional income source. By offering a range of branded merchandise, from clothing to accessories and collectibles, MrBeast not only generates revenue but also solidifies his brand's presence in the minds of his audience.

Merchandising serves as a tangible extension of MrBeast's brand. Each piece of merchandise proudly displays his logo, catchphrases, or iconic imagery. Fans who purchase and wear these items essentially become brand ambassadors, promoting MrBeast's content and values wherever they go.

Moreover, branded merchandise reinforces MrBeast's identity as a creator who values his audience. When fans wear his merchandise, they not only express their support but also feel a deeper connection to the content and community. This emotional bond enhances brand loyalty and encourages viewers to continue engaging with his content.

MrBeast strategically employs the concept of limited edition drops to create a sense of urgency and exclusivity among his fanbase. By releasing a limited quantity of specially designed merchandise for a brief period, he taps into the psychology of scarcity. Fans rush to purchase these items before they sell out, resulting in heightened demand and anticipation.

This approach not only boosts sales but also fosters a sense of belonging among those who manage to acquire the exclusive merchandise. It reinforces the idea that fans are part of an elite club, strengthening their connection to the brand.

Each piece of MrBeast merchandise tells a story. Whether it's a reference to a memorable video challenge or an iconic quote, the merchandise encapsulates the essence of his content. Fans who wear these items become walking storytellers, sparking conversations and interactions based on the narratives behind the designs.

MrBeast occasionally integrates merchandise into his video challenges, adding an interactive element that engages his audience. For example, he might hide golden tickets in select merchandise orders, offering fans the chance to win substantial prizes. This approach not only incentivizes merchandise purchases but also transforms them into exciting experiences for fans.

MrBeast's involvement in the merchandise process goes beyond slapping his name on products. He actively participates in designing and selecting items that resonate with his audience. This personal touch adds authenticity to the merchandise, reinforcing the idea that it's an extension of himself and his content.

Leveraging Data in Marketing

At the core of MrBeast's approach is a commitment to data-driven decision making. He recognizes the value of data in understanding his audience and shaping his content and marketing strategies. This approach involves collecting and analyzing various types of data, such as viewer demographics, watch time, engagement metrics, and more.

One of the key applications of data analytics is audience profiling. MrBeast employs analytics tools to gain a deep understanding of his viewers, including their age, gender, location, and interests. This information helps him create content that resonates with his target demographic.

Analyzing the performance of individual videos is a critical aspect of MrBeast's strategy. He reviews metrics such as view counts, likes, shares, and comments to assess which content resonates most with his audience. By identifying patterns of success, he can replicate and build upon winning formulas.

To refine his content and promotional strategies, MrBeast often conducts A/B testing. This involves creating variations of content or promotional approaches and comparing their performance. A/B testing helps him optimize video titles, thumbnails, descriptions, and marketing campaigns for maximum impact.

The digital landscape is constantly evolving, and MrBeast stays ahead of the curve by monitoring trends. He uses analytics tools to identify emerging topics, keywords, and content formats that are gaining traction. By incorporating these trends into his content, he ensures its relevance and discoverability.

MrBeast understands that engagement is a key factor in YouTube's algorithm. He carefully analyzes viewer engagement data to determine what keeps his audience watching, whether it's a particular segment of a video, an interactive element, or a specific style of content. This knowledge helps him maintain high levels of viewer engagement.

In addition to content analysis, MrBeast applies data insights to his marketing campaigns. He tracks the performance of social media posts, promotional teasers, and collaborations, adjusting strategies based on the data. This ensures that his marketing efforts are effective in generating anticipation and engagement.

Perhaps one of MrBeast's strengths is his agility in adapting to changing circumstances. When he notices shifts in audience behavior or preferences through data analysis, he is quick to pivot his content or marketing approach. This adaptability keeps his brand relevant and engaging.

While data and analytics play a crucial role in MrBeast's strategy, he understands that content creation is also an art. He strikes a balance between the creative aspects of content production and the scientific approach of data analysis, ensuring that his content remains authentic and captivating.

MrBeast Tips for Creators

Recognizing the challenges faced by aspiring YouTubers, MrBeast has shared several valuable tips for upcoming creators looking to find success on the platform:

- Focus on the Beginning of Your Videos: MrBeast emphasizes the importance of telling viewers why they should watch your video right at the start. Avoid beginning with unrelated shots, as the initial moments are crucial in retaining viewers.

- Understanding YouTube's Algorithm: He advises against blaming the algorithm for poor performance. Instead, MrBeast suggests delving into your channel's analytics to understand what works and what doesn't. He emphasizes focusing on Click-Through-Ratios and Viewer Retention as key metrics for success.

- Viewer Satisfaction: Keeping viewers satisfied is critical. MrBeast notes that YouTube's Recommendations team is working on incorporating viewer satisfaction as a factor in recommending videos.

- Evaluating Content: Consider if your content is engaging enough for viewers to watch all the way through and if they will be interested in watching your next video.

- Never a Dull Moment: Ensure that every shot or scene in your video is impactful. Both filming and editing should aim to eliminate dull moments.

- Create a Payoff: Have something at the end of the video that keeps viewers watching the full length.

- Study Your Retention Graph: Look at points where viewers drop off and learn what to avoid in future videos.

- Regular Brainstorming: Spend time each day brainstorming new video ideas or approaches.

- Creating the Right Environment: Cultivate an environment that motivates you to keep working on videos, including the physical workspace and the people you collaborate with.

- Connect with Other Creators: Collaboration can be a key to success, so don't hesitate to work with others.

These tips reflect MrBeast's approach to YouTube, focusing on understanding the platform's mechanics, maintaining high engagement, and continuously improving content quality

Content for Each Platform

MrBeast's marketing brilliance shines through his ability to tailor content and interactions to the unique characteristics of each social media platform. He understands that a one-size-fits-all approach doesn't work in the diverse landscape of digital media. This section delves into how he customizes his content strategy to maximize reach and engagement on various platforms, ultimately driving traffic back to his YouTube channel.

Instagram: Behind-the-Scenes Glimpses

On Instagram, MrBeast offers his audience a behind-the-scenes look into his life and content creation process. He shares candid moments, sneak peeks of upcoming videos, and personal anecdotes. This approach humanizes his brand, making him more relatable to his followers. By allowing his audience to see the person behind the larger-than-life persona, he fosters a sense of connection and authenticity that resonates with Instagram users.

Twitter: Interactive Engagement

Twitter is where MrBeast engages in real-time conversations with his audience. He uses this platform for interactive engagement, hosting Q&A sessions, posing thought-provoking questions, and responding to comments and mentions. By actively participating in conversations and staying up-to-date with trending topics, he keeps his Twitter feed dynamic and engaging.

This approach encourages more significant user participation and sharing of his content.

TikTok: Bite-Sized Entertainment

TikTok is all about short, attention-grabbing content, and MrBeast knows how to captivate its users. He adapts his content for TikTok by condensing his larger projects into bite-sized, highly entertaining videos. These snippets provide a taste of his content while leaving viewers curious for more. This approach leverages the platform's addictive nature and prompts users to explore his YouTube channel for the full experience.

Facebook: Wide Outreach

MrBeast utilizes Facebook's wide-reaching audience by sharing longer-form content, such as highlights from his YouTube videos and in-depth explanations of his philanthropic initiatives. Facebook's diverse user base allows him to reach a broader demographic, and his content is optimized to engage both new and existing fans. By tapping into the potential of Facebook's extensive user network, he expands his brand's visibility and appeals to a more extensive audience.

YouTube Shorts: Short-Form Impact

With the advent of YouTube Shorts, MrBeast embraces this new format to cater to short-form content enthusiasts. He creates concise, impactful videos that are designed specifically for the Shorts platform. These Shorts serve as teasers, enticing viewers to explore his longer YouTube content. By strategically incorporating Shorts into his content strategy, he capitalizes on YouTube's features and algorithms, ensuring that his channel remains at the forefront of recommendations.

Viral Trends and Challenges

MrBeast has demonstrated a remarkable ability to leverage viral trends and challenges to engage his audience and increase his content's visibility. This section of the chapter explores how he harnesses trending topics and viral challenges to his advantage.

MrBeast's approach often begins with identifying emerging viral trends and challenges. He keeps a close eye on popular hashtags, challenges, and memes circulating on social media platforms. By staying attuned to what is capturing the internet's attention, he can conceptualize content that aligns with these trends.

Once MrBeast identifies a relevant trend or challenge, he incorporates it into his content in a creative and engaging manner. Whether it's participating in a viral challenge, creating a unique spin on an existing trend, or even initiating his challenges, he ensures that the content feels both timely and exciting.

One of MrBeast's strengths is his ability to encourage audience participation in these viral campaigns. He designs challenges or activities that viewers can replicate or engage with in some way. This active involvement not only makes his content more relatable but also fosters a sense of community among his audience.

MrBeast's promotional strategies are designed to amplify the reach of his viral content. He encourages viewers to share his videos, challenges, or participation instructions with their friends and social media networks. This organic sharing helps in spreading the content far beyond his existing audience.

Engaging with viral trends and challenges creates a sense of community among MrBeast's viewers. It fosters a collective experience where viewers can connect with each other through shared participation. This community-building aspect strengthens viewer loyalty and encourages them to return for more content.

MrBeast's ability to stay relevant and timely in his content creation is a hallmark of his success with viral trends. He continuously monitors the evolving landscape of viral challenges and adapts his content to align with what is currently trending. This agility allows him to capture the attention of a broad audience.

In the world of digital content, measuring the impact of viral campaigns is essential. MrBeast closely analyzes engagement metrics, such as views, likes, shares, and comments, to gauge the success of his viral content. These insights inform his future content strategies.

Unique and Innovative Content

One of the most defining aspects of MrBeast's content is its inherent blend of entertainment with altruism. His videos frequently feature extravagant giveaways, ranging from substantial monetary rewards to cars and houses. These acts of generosity are not mere stunts; they are carefully crafted to maximize viewer engagement while simultaneously promoting philanthropic causes. For instance, his initiative "Team Trees," co-created with Mark Rober, aimed to plant 20 million trees. The campaign was a resounding success, galvanizing his audience and the wider YouTube community in a collective environmental effort.

Equally significant is the educational element present in his content. While the entertainment value of his videos is indisputable, there is often an underlying educational narrative. This narrative is typically woven into the content subtly yet effectively, ensuring that viewers are not only entertained but also informed. Whether it's discussing environmental issues, promoting scientific understanding, or highlighting social causes, MrBeast finds innovative ways to incorporate educational content into his videos.

Furthermore, MrBeast's content is designed to resonate emotionally with his audience. This emotional connection is fostered not only through the content itself but also through his engaging personality and genuine rapport with his viewers. His approachability and relatable nature have helped cultivate a loyal fanbase that not only consumes his content but also actively participates in his various campaigns and initiatives.

The shareability of his content is another critical factor in his success. MrBeast's videos are crafted to encourage viewers to share them across various social media platforms. This strategy amplifies his reach and, by extension, the impact of his philanthropic efforts. The virality of his content is no accident; it is the result of meticulous planning, creativity, and an acute understanding of social media dynamics.

The YouTube Algorithm

The YouTube algorithm is a complex and constantly evolving system that determines how videos are discovered, recommended, and surfaced to viewers on the platform. Understanding how the YouTube algorithm works is essential for creators aiming to maximize their reach and engagement on the platform. Here's a detailed look at the key factors that influence how videos are recommended to viewers:

Viewer Engagement

- Watch Time: This is a measure of how long viewers watch your video. Longer watch times indicate to YouTube that viewers find your content engaging, which can lead to better visibility on the platform. Creating content that captures and retains viewers' attention throughout is crucial.

- Views: The number of views reflects the popularity and reach of a video. However, views alone don't paint the full picture of engagement; they need to be considered alongside other metrics like watch time.

- Likes, Dislikes, Comments, and Shares: These interactive elements are direct indicators of viewer engagement. Likes and comments particularly signal that viewers are not only watching your content but also engaging with it. Shares indicate that viewers found your content valuable enough to spread it to others, which can significantly boost its visibility.

- Balancing Engagement Factors: It's important to create content that not only attracts views but also encourages viewers to interact with your content and watch it through to the end.

Relevance

- Viewer's Interests: YouTube's algorithm tries to match videos with what it thinks a user wants to see based on their past viewing behavior, including their search history and videos they've previously interacted with.

- Personalization: This aspect ensures that two people with different viewing habits will likely see different recommendations, even if they watch some similar content.

- Targeting Your Audience: To leverage relevance, understand your target audience and create content that aligns with their interests and viewing patterns.

Quality of Content

- Technical Quality: High-definition videos with clear audio are often favored as they provide a better viewing experience. Investing in good filming and sound equipment can positively impact your video's performance.

- Content Quality: This includes how informative, entertaining, or valuable your content is. High-quality content is more likely to be shared and recommended by viewers.

- Editing: Well-edited videos that are free of lengthy pauses, distractions, or irrelevant sections tend to keep viewers engaged longer.

Freshness

- New Content: YouTube often prioritizes new content, particularly if it covers trending topics. Regularly uploading fresh content can increase your channel's visibility.

- Timeliness: Covering current events or trending topics can give your videos a temporary boost in recommendations.

Click-Through Rate (CTR)

- Thumbnail and Title: These are the first things viewers notice. A compelling thumbnail and an intriguing title can significantly improve your CTR.

- Balancing CTR with Watch Time: High CTR is valuable, but if viewers click away quickly, it can negatively impact your video. Aim for a balance between enticing viewers to click and keeping them engaged throughout the video.

Frequency of Uploads

- Consistency: Regularly uploading content can signal to YouTube that your channel is active and constantly providing new material for viewers.

- Schedule: Maintaining a consistent posting schedule can also help build a loyal audience, as viewers know when to expect new content from you.

User Feedback

- Direct Interaction: Tools like surveys or the "not interested" feature give YouTube direct feedback from viewers about their content preferences.

- Adapting to Feedback: Pay attention to these signals to understand what your audience prefers and dislikes.

Creator and Channel Authority

- Subscriber Count and Viewership: Channels with a large number of subscribers and consistent viewership are often seen as authoritative and trustworthy by the algorithm.

- Content History: A history of creating popular, high-quality content can also give channels an edge in recommendations.

Succeeding on YouTube involves a combination of creating high-quality, engaging content that resonates with your target audience and understanding the nuances of how the YouTube algorithm works. Balancing these elements effectively can lead to increased visibility and success on the platform.

Daily Masterminds

The Daily Masterminds played a pivotal role in MrBeast's journey to becoming one of the most prominent and influential creators on YouTube. This collaborative group, consisting of MrBeast and fellow aspiring YouTubers, had a significant impact on his success. Here, we delve into the role of Daily Masterminds in shaping MrBeast's career:

The Daily Masterminds was a collective of content creators who came together with a shared goal: to analyze and understand the intricacies of successful YouTube videos. This group was formed organically, with members dedicated to exploring the strategies, trends, and techniques used by popular YouTubers to engage and captivate their audiences.

Meetings were characterized by long and intensive sessions where members dissected the content of renowned YouTubers. These sessions were not merely about criticism but focused on deep analysis and learning. Participants would discuss various elements, such as video structure, storytelling techniques, editing styles, and audience engagement strategies.

One of the primary objectives of these collaborative sessions was to identify the key factors that contributed to the success of certain YouTube videos and channels. By studying successful creators' content, Daily Masterminds members gained insights into what resonated with viewers and how to replicate those elements in their own work.

Daily Masterminds instilled a culture of continuous learning and adaptation. MrBeast and his fellow members recognized the ever-evolving nature of YouTube and digital content creation. This mindset encouraged them to experiment with new ideas, incorporate successful strategies into their videos, and stay ahead of emerging trends in the platform's algorithm.

Beyond analysis and strategy discussions, the Daily Masterminds provided a support system for its members. Collaboration and mutual encouragement were essential aspects of the group's dynamics. Members motivated each other to persevere through challenges and setbacks, fostering a sense of community and shared goals.

MrBeast's active participation in the Daily Masterminds had a direct impact on his content strategy. He applied the knowledge gained from these collaborative sessions to his videos, making them more engaging and effective. This strategic approach, combined with his dedication, helped propel his channel to new heights.

The Daily Masterminds played a crucial role in MrBeast's rise to fame. It provided him with a competitive edge by allowing him to incorporate successful strategies into his content. The group's culture of constant learning and adaptation became a fundamental part of his content creation process, enabling him to consistently engage and entertain his audience.

Strategic Audience Engagement

MrBeast (Jimmy Donaldson) has been successful in engaging a global audience on YouTube, not just through his content but also through strategic audience engagement and localization efforts. From the beginning of his YouTube career, MrBeast has been focused on understanding viewer behavior, analyzing when viewers tend to stop watching his videos and what makes thumbnails effective in attracting clicks. This approach has been crucial in tailoring his content to maximize viewer retention and engagement.

MrBeast's strategy includes localizing his content for international audiences, which has significantly expanded his reach. He has created separate channels for different languages, like Spanish, Russian, Portuguese, and French, and hired native speakers to provide voice-overs for his videos. This effort in dubbing and localization has paid off immensely, as seen in the first half of 2022, where his localized channel views totaled over 160 million. This approach demonstrates his understanding that localization is more than translation; it's about appealing to the nuances of different cultures.

Moreover, MrBeast has shared insights on the importance of video thumbnails in attracting viewers. He emphasizes that thumbnails should clearly depict what viewers can expect in the video and align with the video title. He also recommends creating a few variations of thumbnails for each video, allowing for quick changes if a particular thumbnail does not perform as expected. This attention to detail in thumbnail design has proven to be a critical factor in the success of his videos.

He pays close attention to viewer retention rates, noting the points in his videos where viewers tend to drop off. This analysis helps him understand which parts of his content are most engaging and which parts might need rethinking. He also assesses the effectiveness of his video thumbnails and titles, evaluating their click-through rates (CTR). A high CTR indicates a compelling thumbnail and title, but it's the retention rate that tells him if the content lived up to the viewer's expectations set by the thumbnail.

This data-centric approach has been pivotal in enabling MrBeast to tailor his content to maximize viewer retention and engagement. He understands that on YouTube, it's not just about the number of views a video gets; it's about how long it can keep viewers engaged. This understanding shapes every aspect of his content creation process, from conceptualization to execution.

The insights gleaned from this ongoing analysis have significantly influenced MrBeast's content strategy. He has an uncanny ability to pinpoint precisely what captivates his audience and consistently incorporates these elements into his videos. For instance, MrBeast is known for his extravagant challenges and philanthropic endeavors, which are not only entertaining but also resonate with his audience's love for engaging, high-stakes content.

MrBeast's content creation is far from being a shot in the dark; it is a calculated response to audience preferences and trends. He keeps his finger on the pulse of what's current and popular, ensuring his content stays relevant and engaging. This responsiveness to audience trends is complemented by his creativity and willingness to push boundaries, making his content both unique and in tune with viewer interests.

Diversified Revenue Streams

MrBeast, renowned for his innovative content creation, has established a diverse array of revenue streams that contribute to his financial success. His primary income sources include YouTube ad revenue, brand sponsorships, and merchandise sales, along with various business ventures.

YouTube Ad Revenue: MrBeast's main YouTube channel alone is estimated to generate between $2.5 million to $40 million per year, contributing significantly to his total earnings. Across his different channels, such as

Beast Reacts, Gaming, and MrBeast 2, his annual YouTube income is approximately $50 million.

Brand Sponsorships: In addition to YouTube ads, MrBeast has secured several high-paying brand sponsorship deals. These partnerships have included companies like Honey, Quidd, Electronic Arts, and MSCHF. The rates for these sponsorships vary, but they are estimated to bring in around $10-20 million per year. This income stream is crucial for MrBeast, as it provides a substantial amount of his revenue.

Merchandise Sales: Selling branded merchandise, including t-shirts, hoodies, hats, water bottles, and other items, is another lucrative source of income for MrBeast. His merchandise sales, including collaborations with brands for limited-run products, likely generate around $5 million annually. This merchandise strategy capitalizes on his brand and fanbase, offering an additional revenue stream beyond digital content.

Other Business Ventures: MrBeast has expanded his income sources through various business ventures. These include his delivery-only virtual restaurant chain, MrBeast Burger, which has grown to over 1,000 locations, and Beast Philanthropy, his registered nonprofit for philanthropic initiatives. Additionally, he has invested in Creative Juice, a production company. These ventures contribute at least another $5 million or more to his annual income.

Content Creation and Marketing: MrBeast's success is not only due to his diverse revenue streams but also his approach to content creation and marketing. His videos are known for their unique and engaging content, combining philanthropy, entertainment, and education. He utilizes eye-catching thumbnails and engaging titles to attract viewers, ensuring his content remains both relevant and popular.

MrBeast's income is a result of his multifaceted approach, combining content creation, strategic partnerships, and entrepreneurship. His ability to diversify his revenue streams and consistently deliver engaging content has solidified his position as one of the most successful YouTubers and digital entrepreneurs.

Expanding Digital Presence

MrBeast has effectively expanded his digital presence beyond YouTube, solidifying his brand and engaging a broader audience across various platforms. His multi-platform presence is a crucial aspect of his business model, allowing him to reach and interact with diverse audience segments.

Diverse Customer Segments: MrBeast's content caters to a global YouTube audience, including specific sub-segments like gamers (through MrBeast Gaming), food enthusiasts (MrBeast Burger), and philanthropists/environmentalists (Team Trees and

Team Seas). This approach ensures his brand remains relevant and continues to grow, appealing to various interests and demographics.

Expanding Across Digital Platforms: In addition to his primary presence on YouTube, MrBeast has diversified across other digital platforms, including Instagram, Twitter, TikTok, and Snapchat. This expansion enables him to share content, updates, promotions, and interact with his community on their preferred platforms, enhancing his brand presence and engagement.

Exclusive Distribution Deals: MrBeast signed an exclusive multi-year deal with Jellysmack to distribute his YouTube content on Facebook and Snapchat. Jellysmack optimizes content for different social media sites, increasing the creator's presence and fanbase on additional video platforms, thus leading to increased revenue from the additional viewership on these platforms.

Offline Channels and Experiences: Beyond digital channels, MrBeast has experimented with offline channels like pop-up restaurants, namely MrBeast Burger. These ventures not only serve as an additional revenue stream but also offer unique, in-person brand experiences for customers.

Engaging and Building Customer Relationships: Through his engaging content and commitment to social causes, MrBeast has built strong relationships with his audience. He actively engages with them on social media platforms, incorporating their feedback and ideas into his videos. This approach has fostered a loyal community of followers who actively engage with his content and support his initiatives.

Revenue Streams and Business Model: MrBeast's primary revenue streams include advertising revenue from YouTube, brand partnerships and sponsorships, merchandise sales, and income from business ventures like MrBeast Burger. His ability to attract high-profile sponsors and advertisers has grown with his audience, capitalizing on his popularity and reach.

Key Resources and Activities: MrBeast's success relies on his team of content creators, marketers, and business strategists, who produce innovative content and manage various revenue streams and partnerships. His intellectual property, including unique content formats, brand name, and logo, is a vital resource for his brand identity and success.

MrBeast's expansion across multiple digital platforms and his foray into offline experiences demonstrate his versatile approach to audience engagement and brand building. His strategic use of various channels, coupled with his innovative content and business acumen, has cemented his position as a leading figure in the digital content creation space.

Innovative Approaches to Content and Business

MrBeast's early years on YouTube were characterized by modest success, with his audience growing slowly. Initially focused on gaming videos, he gradually transitioned to challenge-based content, which resonated more with a wider audience. His content often featured money and charities, bringing a game-like feel to his videos. This shift in content strategy played a significant role in his rise to fame.

His diverse revenue streams are a critical aspect of his success. In 2021, MrBeast earned $54 million through his YouTube channel, showcasing his ability to monetize his content effectively. Besides his successful YouTube career, MrBeast has ventured into several businesses, including the take-out restaurant MrBeast Burger (with over 1,600 affiliated franchisees), a candy bar brand called Feastables, and his merchandise line. These ventures demonstrate his entrepreneurial spirit and ability to leverage his brand beyond digital content.

MrBeast's approach to content creation sets him apart from other YouTubers. He invests heavily in his productions, focusing on quality over quantity. His videos are known for their large-scale and high-budget production values, like his own version of "The Squid Game," which reportedly cost around $4 million. This investment in high-quality content has allowed him to create a unique viewer experience and amass a massive audience.

One of MrBeast's key strengths is his focus on audience engagement and satisfaction. He meticulously analyzes data such as viewer drop-off points and thumbnail click-through rates to understand what resonates with his audience. This analytical approach has helped him refine his content strategy and increase viewer engagement.

MrBeast's journey highlights the importance of scaling based on intuition and understanding the intricacies of the platform. His ability to apply the principles he learned about content creation on a larger scale has been instrumental in his growth. He has managed to create a team that shares his mindset and vision, allowing him to produce content efficiently while maintaining his role as the central figure.

MrBeast's success story is a blend of creative content creation, strategic audience engagement, innovative business ventures, and a deep understanding of digital platforms. His journey from a young YouTuber to a business mogul exemplifies the power of innovation and adaptation in the digital era. His approach serves as a blueprint for aspiring content creators and entrepreneurs looking to make a significant impact in the digital world.

Strategic Partnerships

One of his notable partnerships is with Shopify. MrBeast collaborated with Shopify to streamline his online merchandise store, leading to a significant boost in sales. This collaboration utilized Shopify's ecommerce expertise to enhance MrBeast's merchandising operations, resulting in increased visibility and profitability for both parties. The success of this partnership lies in its simple yet effective strategy of combining MrBeast's popularity with Shopify's technological capabilities, revolutionizing influencer-based merchandise sales.

In another strategic move, MrBeast teamed up with Hasbro for the NERF brand, launching a social content campaign and working on a NERF blaster collaboration. This 2-year partnership aligns one of YouTube's most-viewed creators with a leading brand in action-based performance toys. The collaboration not only enhances brand visibility but also involves MrBeast in product development, blending his creative input with NERF's product innovation.

MrBeast has also entered into a partnership with Samsung. This collaboration uses Samsung's Galaxy devices, including the Galaxy S23 Ultra, Galaxy Z Flip5, and Galaxy Z Fold5, to create high-quality content for MrBeast's YouTube channel. This partnership aligns MrBeast's content creation expertise with Samsung's cutting-edge technology, demonstrating the potential of mobile devices in high-level content production.

Additionally, MrBeast's collaborations extend into the gaming world, with a partnership with "Stumble Guys," a popular mobile game. This collaboration involves creating experiences within the game that resonate with MrBeast's unique content style, aiming to engage and expand both brands' audiences.

Furthermore, MrBeast has made history with the Charlotte Hornets, marking the first-ever collaboration between a creator-led brand and an NBA franchise. This partnership involves promoting his chocolate bar company, Feastables, on the basketball team's uniform and media backdrops, thereby introducing MrBeast's brand to a new audience and blending the worlds of digital content creation and sports marketing.

These strategic partnerships reflect MrBeast's ability to leverage his influence across various industries, blending content creation with business acumen. Each collaboration not only amplifies his brand's reach but also innovates in the respective fields, showcasing his versatility as a content creator and entrepreneur.

The YouTuber Success Model

In the upcoming sections, we will delve into various facets of the YouTuber success model. From pinpointing your niche and comprehending your audience to mastering content creation and audience engagement, each segment provides invaluable insights and practical strategies. We'll also explore the realms of branding, marketing, and leveraging social media to illuminate the path towards expanding your reach and nurturing a devoted community.

This information is tailored to guide you through the intricacies of cultivating a prosperous YouTube career. In today's digital landscape, YouTube has transformed into a fiercely competitive platform where content creators aspire to attain success. This guide is aimed at dissecting the pivotal elements that contribute to YouTuber success, drawing inspiration from industry luminaries like MrBeast, who have reshaped the landscape of content creation and digital entrepreneurship.

Finding Your Niche

Discovering your niche is a fundamental step towards unlocking the door to success. This chapter delves into the intricate process of finding that unique niche, a journey that demands introspection and keen observation. It's a voyage that calls for a deep understanding of your personal strengths and interests, as well as a sharp awareness of the gaps and opportunities within the vast YouTube ecosystem.

At its core, discovering your niche is about aligning your passions and expertise with the needs and desires of your target audience. It's a deliberate quest to identify that special intersection where your authentic enthusiasm meets the unmet demands of viewers. This journey begins with self-reflection, urging you to ponder what truly ignites your passion and curiosity. It challenges you to uncover subjects that you could discuss endlessly, not out of external pressure, but driven by an inner fire of genuine interest.

However, niche discovery extends beyond introspection. It involves a meticulous exploration of the YouTube content landscape. This exploration includes a thorough examination of existing content, trends, and audience preferences. By navigating the YouTube cosmos with a discerning eye, you can identify areas that are underserved or ripe for innovative approaches. It's akin to becoming an astute observer of constellations, where each trend and audience need forms a unique star in the YouTube universe.

Ultimately, your goal is to craft a Unique Selling Proposition (USP) that sets you apart. This USP might manifest as a distinctive perspective on common themes, a unique presentation style, or an innovative content format. It represents the promise you make to your audience, the offering that entices them to engage with your content, and the voice that resonates uniquely in the YouTube community.

As you embark on this journey of niche discovery, remember that it's not just about finding a place in the YouTube ecosystem; it's about creating your own space, a constellation that shines brilliantly, guides your creative journey, and leaves a lasting impression in the digital universe. So, prepare to embark on this voyage of self-discovery and creative exploration as we navigate the YouTube cosmos to unveil your unique niche.

Unleashing Your Passion

Step 1: Self-Reflection and Introspection

The journey of discovering your niche on YouTube begins with a profound exploration of your personal passions and interests. This introspective journey is not a mere formality but a vital foundation upon which your entire YouTube career will be built.

Start by setting aside dedicated time for self-reflection. Find a quiet space where you can think, ponder, and delve deep into your innermost thoughts. Consider the following questions:

- What subjects or topics am I genuinely passionate about?

- What are the activities that bring me immense joy and satisfaction?

- In which domains do my natural talents and abilities naturally shine?

These questions are not meant to be answered hastily. Take your time to think deeply, and don't be afraid to revisit them periodically as your interests and passions evolve over time.

Step 2: Identify Endless Conversations

One hallmark of a true passion is the ability to engage in endless conversations about a particular subject. Think about the topics or subjects that you can discuss for hours on end without feeling bored or exhausted. These are the subjects that hold a special place in your heart, and they are often the foundation of a successful YouTube niche.

Consider the following:

- Are there specific hobbies or interests that you could talk about non-stop?

- Do you find yourself drawn to certain discussions, debates, or conversations more than others?

- Are there subjects that have consistently piqued your curiosity over the years?

By identifying these topics, you'll be uncovering potential areas for your YouTube content that align with your genuine passions.

Step 3: Seek Unbridled Joy

Authenticity in content creation is rooted in genuine enthusiasm. Take a moment to reflect on the activities or pursuits that bring you unbridled joy. These are the moments when you feel most alive, invigorated, and completely absorbed in the experience.

Ask yourself:

- What activities or hobbies do I engage in that make me forget about time and space?

- When do I feel the most fulfilled and content?

- Are there particular moments or experiences that have left a lasting impression on me?

These moments of unbridled joy often point towards areas where you can create content that resonates deeply with your audience because your enthusiasm will shine through in every video.

Step 4: Embrace Your Natural Talents

Each of us possesses unique talents and abilities that set us apart. Consider the domains in which you excel effortlessly or the skills that you have developed over time. Your innate talents can be a guiding light in your niche discovery process.

Reflect on:

- What skills do I naturally possess that could be valuable in content creation?

- Are there areas where others often seek my advice or guidance?

- Can I leverage my talents to create content that stands out from the crowd?

By embracing your natural talents, you not only ensure that you're creating content authentically but also leveraging your strengths to captivate your audience.

Step 5: The Authenticity Imperative

Throughout this introspective journey, keep in mind that authenticity is the bedrock of successful content creation on YouTube. Viewers have a discerning eye, and they can readily distinguish between genuine enthusiasm and feigned interest.

Your passion, joy, and talents should align authentically with your chosen niche. If you genuinely love what you're creating and it aligns with your interests, your audience will be drawn to your authentic approach.

Discovering your niche on YouTube is a deeply introspective journey that revolves around understanding your passions, identifying topics that ignite endless conversations, seeking joy in your interests, and embracing your natural talents. By embarking on this introspective quest, you lay the foundation for authentic content creation that will resonate with your audience and pave the way for a successful YouTube career. Remember, your passion is your compass on this journey, guiding you toward a niche that reflects your authentic self.

Define a Gap

In this section, we will provide steps to analyze the YouTube content landscape, helping you identify potential niche opportunities for your channel.

Step 1: Define Your Niche

Before delving into the analysis of gaps in YouTube content, it's essential to have a clear definition of your niche. Your niche is the specific area or subject matter that your YouTube channel will focus on. It should align with your personal interests and passions, as discussed in the previous chapter. Once you have a well-defined niche, you can proceed with the analysis.

Step 2: Study Existing Content

Start by immersing yourself in the existing content within your chosen niche. Watch videos, read articles, and engage with communities related to your niche. Gain a comprehensive understanding of the content landscape, including the key creators, popular trends, and common themes. Take notes on what works well and what could be improved.

Step 3: Identify Popular Creators

Identify the creators who have a significant presence within your niche. Analyze their content to understand what makes them successful. Pay attention to their content style, production quality, and engagement with their audience. Take note of the topics and angles they frequently cover.

Step 4: Recognize Oversaturation

Within your chosen niche, there may be areas that are oversaturated with content creators. These are topics or sub-niches where numerous creators are vying for attention, making it challenging for newcomers to stand out. Identify these oversaturated areas within your niche as they may not be the best starting point for your YouTube journey.

Step 5: Explore Underrepresented Areas

Simultaneously, search for underrepresented areas or niches within your broader niche. These are topics or subtopics that have not received as much attention or high-quality content on YouTube. Look for gaps where there is an audience interested in the subject, but limited or subpar content exists. These underrepresented areas hold potential opportunities for you to make your mark.

Step 6: Analyze Audience Demand

Research and analyze audience demand within your niche. Use keyword research tools, social media listening, and surveys to understand what questions, problems, or topics your potential audience is searching for. Identify the pain points and interests of your target viewers, as this will guide your content creation strategy.

Step 7: Assess Competition

Assess the competition in both oversaturated and underrepresented areas of your niche. Determine the level of competition, the quality of content being produced, and the engagement of their audiences. Competition can provide insights into the challenges and opportunities within your niche.

Step 8: Consider Your Unique Perspective

As you analyze gaps in YouTube content, consider how your unique perspective and interests can fill those gaps. Think about how you can approach topics differently, offer a fresh angle, or provide a unique value proposition to your audience. Your authentic voice and perspective can be a differentiating factor in a competitive landscape.

Step 9: Validate Your Niche Choice

Based on your analysis, validate your niche choice. Ensure that it aligns with your passions and interests, and that there are opportunities for you to create valuable content within that niche. Remember that a well-researched and strategically chosen niche is more likely to lead to long-term success on YouTube.

Step 10: Prepare Your Content Strategy

Armed with a deep understanding of your niche and the gaps you intend to fill, start crafting your content strategy. Outline the types of videos you will create, the topics you will cover, and the unique angles or approaches you will take. Your content strategy should be informed by the insights gained during your gap analysis.

Analyzing gaps in YouTube content is a crucial step in finding your niche and shaping your content strategy. It requires a thorough examination of the existing content landscape, identification of oversaturated and underrepresented areas, and a deep understanding of audience demand. By conducting this meticulous gap analysis, you can position yourself to create content that stands out and resonates with your target audience. Your niche discovery journey is now guided not only by your passions but also by strategic insights into the YouTube universe.

Crafting Your Unique Selling Proposition (USP)

In the intricate journey of YouTube content creation, discovering your niche is just the beginning. The next pivotal step is to transform that niche into a captivating and irresistible Unique Selling Proposition (USP). Your USP is the essence of what sets your content apart, making it unique and alluring to a specific audience segment. This chapter delves into the intricacies of crafting a compelling USP that will serve as your guiding star, ensuring that your content shines brilliantly in the crowded digital panorama.

Step 1: Understand Your Niche

Before crafting your USP, it's essential to have a deep understanding of your chosen niche. Delve into the nuances of the subject matter, explore the existing content landscape, and identify the prevailing trends and audience expectations. This foundational knowledge will serve as the canvas upon which you'll paint your unique content proposition.

Step 2: Identify Your Unique Perspective

A distinctive USP often arises from a unique perspective on commonplace topics. Ask yourself what perspective, angle, or viewpoint you can bring to your niche that sets you apart from others. Perhaps it's a fresh take, a contrarian viewpoint, or a personal connection that makes your perspective special. Your unique viewpoint forms the cornerstone of your USP.

Step 3: Explore Innovative Presentation Styles

Innovation in presentation style can be a powerful component of your USP. Consider how you can package your content differently from the norm. This might involve experimenting with storytelling techniques, visual aesthetics, or interactive elements that engage your audience in new and exciting ways. Think outside the box and explore presentation styles that resonate with your niche and audience.

Step 4: Embrace Uncharted Formats

To truly stand out, consider adopting formats that remain largely unexplored within your niche. Whether it's a specific video structure, a recurring segment, or a unique series concept, the goal is to offer something fresh and exciting. Research your niche to uncover uncharted territories and be the pioneer who introduces a novel format to your audience.

Step 5: Cater to Your Audience's Desires

Your USP should align with the desires and preferences of your target audience. Take the time to understand what your viewers seek from content within your niche. Conduct surveys, read comments, and engage with your audience to gain insights into their needs and expectations. Tailor your USP to cater to these desires, ensuring that it resonates strongly with your viewers.

Step 6: Consistency is Key

Consistency in delivering your USP is paramount. Viewers should come to expect a certain quality, style, or perspective when they watch your content. Your USP should be the thread that ties your videos together, creating a cohesive and recognizable brand.

Step 7: Iterate and Evolve

As you embark on your content creation journey with your USP in hand, be open to iteration and evolution. Your USP may evolve over time as you gather feedback and gain a deeper understanding of your audience. Embrace change when necessary while staying true to the core elements that make your USP unique.

Crafting a compelling Unique Selling Proposition (USP) is an integral step in your YouTube content creation journey. It's about leveraging your niche, unique perspective, innovative presentation, and uncharted formats to offer something that no one else does or does in a way that is markedly superior or distinct. Your USP serves as the guiding star, ensuring that your content stands out brilliantly in the vast digital landscape.

The journey of discovering one's niche on YouTube is a multifaceted process that amalgamates personal passion, meticulous research, and a fervent commitment to delivering unparalleled value to the audience. It embodies the essence of authenticity and innovation in content creation, and it lays the cornerstone for a successful and fulfilling YouTube career. As we proceed further, we will delve deeper into each facet of this exhilarating expedition, guiding you toward the realization of your YouTube dreams.

Content Creation and Quality

This chapter is dedicated to unraveling the intricacies of content creation and quality, essential elements that shape the trajectory of a YouTube influencer's career, just as they have for MrBeast. We'll explore how balancing authenticity, professionalism, and a commitment to constant evolution can set the stage for a content creator's triumph on the YouTube stage.

Elevating Your Content: The Power of High Production Value

Step 1: Acknowledge the Significance

The journey towards creating exceptional content begins with a fundamental acknowledgment of the paramount importance of high production value. In today's digital era, where content choices abound, the quality of video and audio can make or break viewer engagement and retention.

Step 2: Understand Your Tools

To embark on this quest, you must first acquaint yourself with the tools of the trade. Delve into the nuances of camera quality, exploring different camera options and understanding how they impact the visual appeal of your content. Learn to differentiate between varying microphone setups and grasp the significance of sound clarity in conveying your message effectively. Familiarize yourself with lighting techniques that can transform the ambiance of your videos, setting the mood and capturing your audience's attention.

Step 3: The Art of Meticulous Editing

One of the cornerstones of high production value is the art of meticulous editing. Dive deep into the world of video editing software, mastering its intricacies. Learn to cut, trim, and arrange your footage to create a seamless and engaging narrative. Understand the power of transitions, effects, and color correction to enhance the visual appeal of your content. Embrace the art of storytelling through editing, where every cut and transition contributes to the overall impact of your video.

Step 4: Start with What You Have

While the pursuit of high production value is essential, it's equally vital to recognize that many creators commence their YouTube journeys with basic equipment. Don't let limited resources deter you from embarking on your content creation voyage. Begin with what you have, understanding that the quality of your content can evolve over time. Quality content transcends equipment limitations, and it's your creativity and dedication that will shine through, even in the early stages.

Step 5: Invest in Progress

As your YouTube journey progresses and your audience grows, consider investing in higher-quality tools and equipment. This step is a natural progression in your pursuit of superior production. Upgrading your camera, microphone, lighting setup, and editing software can elevate the overall quality of your content. Your audience will appreciate the enhanced visual and auditory experience, and it positions you as a professional in your field.

Step 6: Consistency and Reliability

Consistency is the bedrock upon which your content creation empire is built. High production value should not be a one-time effort but a consistent commitment. Establish a production routine that ensures each video meets the standards of excellence you've set. Reliability in delivering quality content builds trust with your audience and keeps them coming back for more.

Step 7: Seek Feedback and Learn

Finally, never stop seeking feedback and learning. Engage with your audience to understand their preferences and expectations. Pay attention to comments, messages, and analytics data to identify areas for improvement. Attend workshops, courses, or join online communities to stay updated with the latest production techniques and trends.

By understanding the significance of quality video and audio, mastering your tools, embracing meticulous editing, and investing in your equipment over time, you can position yourself as a professional content creator. Your commitment to excellence will not only enhance viewer engagement and retention but also reflect your respect for your audience's time and attention. Remember, every step you take towards high production value is a step closer to leaving a lasting impact in the digital landscape.

Authenticity and Professionalism: Creating Meaningful Connections

Step 1: Understanding the Balance

The journey of content creation on YouTube often requires creators to navigate the delicate balance between authenticity and professionalism. Striking this balance is essential for fostering meaningful connections with viewers and building credibility and trust.

Step 2: Embrace Your Authentic Self

Authenticity is the cornerstone of any successful YouTube channel. Start by embracing your authentic self and being genuine in your content. Authenticity shines through in your words, actions, and the way you present yourself on camera. It's about being real, honest, and transparent with your audience. Share your thoughts, experiences, and opinions sincerely.

Step 3: Scripting vs. Spontaneity

One of the key considerations in balancing authenticity and professionalism is the choice between scripting and spontaneity. Some creators prefer scripted content to ensure precision and clarity, while others thrive on spontaneous, off-the-cuff delivery. Understand your own style and what works best for your content. You can strike a balance by scripting key points or outlines while allowing room for authentic, unscripted moments that connect with your audience on a personal level.

Step 4: Maintain a Consistent Brand Voice

Consistency is crucial in building a recognizable brand on YouTube. Establish and maintain a consistent brand voice that aligns with your values and resonates with your audience. Whether you're creating educational content, entertainment, or vlogs, your brand voice should reflect your personality and style. This consistency reinforces your authenticity while presenting a professional image.

Step 5: Relatability and Respect

Being relatable to your audience is a powerful way to connect authentically. Share relatable experiences, stories, and challenges that your viewers can relate to. However, remember the importance of respect. While being authentic and relatable, avoid crossing boundaries or offending your audience. Strive for a balance where you maintain a friendly, approachable demeanor while upholding a level of professionalism and respect.

Step 6: Engage with Your Audience

Engagement is a vital aspect of authenticity and professionalism. Respond to comments, messages, and social media interactions from your audience. Show that you value their input and appreciate their support. Genuine engagement fosters a sense of community and connection.

Step 7: Learn from Feedback

Feedback from your audience can provide valuable insights into striking the right balance. Pay attention to constructive criticism and suggestions. Use feedback to refine your content, presentation style, and approach to ensure you maintain authenticity while enhancing professionalism.

Step 8: Evolve and Adapt

The balance between authenticity and professionalism is not static; it evolves over time. As you grow and learn, your approach may change. Be open to adaptation and refinement in response to audience feedback and changing trends. Authenticity and professionalism can coexist harmoniously when they are in sync with your growth as a content creator.

By embracing your authentic self, making thoughtful choices between scripting and spontaneity, maintaining a consistent brand voice, and engaging with your audience, you can create meaningful connections while upholding professionalism. Remember that finding the right balance is an ongoing process that evolves as you grow as a content creator. It is through this balance that you can establish trust, build a loyal audience, and make a lasting impact in the YouTube community.

Adapting and Evolving: The Art of Staying Relevant

Step 1: Embrace Change

To thrive in the ever-evolving digital landscape, content creators must first embrace the idea that change is inevitable. The first step in adapting and evolving content is accepting that audience preferences, trends, and technology are in a constant state of flux. Being open to change is the foundation upon which you can build a strategy for staying relevant.

Step 2: Monitor Trends and Audience Preferences

Staying attuned to current trends and understanding shifting audience preferences is pivotal. Dedicate time to research and keep a close eye on emerging trends within your niche. Engage with your audience through comments, surveys, and social media to gain insights into their evolving interests and needs. Trends and preferences can guide you in shaping your content strategy.

Step 3: Analyze Analytics and Feedback

Your YouTube analytics and audience feedback are invaluable resources for evolution. Regularly analyze your video performance metrics, including watch time, click-through rates, and audience retention. Identify patterns and trends in your data to understand which content resonates most with your viewers. Pay attention to comments and messages from your audience to gain qualitative insights and feedback.

Step 4: Experiment with Fresh Ideas

Experimentation is the heart of evolution. Don't be afraid to step out of your comfort zone and try new content formats, styles, or topics. Test different approaches and ideas to gauge their reception with your audience. Experimentation is not limited to content; it can also include changes in video length, posting frequency, or even the platforms you use to engage with your audience.

Step 5: Stay Informed and Educated

The digital landscape is ever-changing, and staying informed is key to adaptation. Continuously educate yourself about the latest tools, techniques, and trends in content creation. Attend workshops, conferences, and webinars related to your niche. Follow industry leaders and subscribe to channels or websites that provide updates on digital marketing and content creation.

Step 6: Collaborate and Network

Collaboration and networking can open doors to fresh perspectives and ideas. Partner with other creators in your niche or related fields to collaborate on projects or exchange insights. Networking with fellow creators, industry professionals, and even your audience can provide diverse viewpoints and opportunities for growth.

Step 7: Evolution with Purpose

While adapting and evolving is crucial, ensure that your changes align with your channel's core identity and purpose. Evolution should not compromise your authenticity or alienate your existing audience. Strike a balance between staying true to your brand while incorporating necessary adaptations.

Step 8: Consistency Amidst Evolution

Consistency remains a foundational element in content creation. As you evolve, maintain a level of consistency in your content style, release schedule, and brand voice. This consistency provides a sense of reliability for your audience, even as you adapt to changing trends.

Step 9: Learn from Failures

Not every experiment or adaptation will yield positive results. Embrace failures as opportunities for learning and growth. Analyze what went wrong, gather insights from feedback, and use these experiences to refine your future content strategies.

Step 10: Iterate and Repeat

Adaptation and evolution are iterative processes. Regularly revisit your content strategy, analyze results, gather feedback, and make adjustments accordingly. The journey of staying relevant is ongoing, and creators who embrace continuous improvement are more likely to thrive in the dynamic digital landscape.

Adapting and evolving content is a vital aspect of content creation on YouTube. By embracing change, monitoring trends, analyzing analytics and feedback, experimenting with fresh ideas, staying informed, collaborating, and maintaining consistency, creators can keep their content relevant and engaging in an ever-changing digital world. Evolution should be purposeful, aligned with your brand identity, and driven by a commitment to providing value to your audience. Through this commitment to growth and adaptation, creators can build lasting connections and remain at the forefront of their niche.

Learning and Growing with Technology

Step 1: Recognize the Importance of Technology

The first step in learning and growing with technology is acknowledging its pivotal role in content creation. Understand that technology is not merely a tool but an enabler that can elevate your content quality, expand your reach, and strengthen your connection with the audience. Embrace the mindset that staying updated with the latest tools and techniques is essential for success in the digital landscape.

Step 2: Invest in Quality Equipment

Begin by investing in quality equipment. This includes cameras, microphones, lighting setups, and computer hardware. Research and select equipment that aligns with your content goals and budget. Quality equipment enhances the visual and auditory aspects of your content, contributing to a professional and engaging viewer experience.

Step 3: Master Video Editing Software

Video editing software is a cornerstone of content creation. Learn to use professional video editing tools to enhance your videos. Invest time in mastering software like Adobe Premiere Pro, Final Cut Pro, or DaVinci Resolve. These tools allow you to edit, refine, and enhance your footage, creating polished and compelling content.

Step 4: Explore Graphic Design Tools

Graphic design plays a significant role in branding and visual appeal. Familiarize yourself with graphic design software such as Adobe Photoshop, Canva, or Adobe Illustrator. These tools enable you to create eye-catching thumbnails, channel art, and graphics that resonate with your audience and reinforce your brand identity.

Step 5: Leverage Social Media Platforms

Social media platforms are powerful tools for content promotion and audience engagement. Create and maintain a presence on platforms like Instagram, Twitter, Facebook, and TikTok. Share behind-the-scenes content, teasers, and updates to connect with your audience beyond YouTube. Engage with your audience, respond to comments, and foster a sense of community.

Step 6: Stay Informed and Educated

Technology evolves rapidly, so staying informed is essential. Follow industry news, blogs, and YouTube channels that focus on technology and content creation. Participate in online forums and communities where creators discuss the latest tools and techniques. Attend webinars, workshops, and online courses to expand your knowledge and skills.

Step 7: Collaborate and Network

Collaboration and networking can provide valuable insights into technology trends and innovations. Collaborate with other creators, especially those who specialize in technology or related fields. Networking with professionals and experts in the tech and content creation industries can lead to valuable partnerships and knowledge sharing.

Step 8: Experiment and Innovate

Don't hesitate to experiment with new technologies and techniques. Test different camera angles, explore 360-degree videos, or experiment with virtual reality. Innovate your content by embracing emerging technologies like live streaming, augmented reality, or interactive storytelling. Audiences often appreciate creators who push the boundaries of technology.

Step 9: Prioritize Accessibility

As you embrace technology, remember to prioritize accessibility. Ensure that your content is accessible to a broad audience, including those with disabilities. Learn about closed captions, audio descriptions, and accessible design principles to make your content inclusive and user-friendly.

Step 10: Continuously Evolve

Technology is ever-evolving, and so should your knowledge and skills. Embrace a mindset of continuous learning and growth. Regularly evaluate your tech stack, update software and equipment, and adapt to new technologies that can enhance your content creation process and audience engagement.

Learning and growing with technology is a fundamental aspect of content creation in the digital age. By investing in quality equipment, mastering video editing and graphic design software, leveraging social media, staying informed and educated, collaborating and networking, experimenting with new technologies, prioritizing accessibility, and maintaining a mindset of continuous evolution, creators can harness the power of technology to create compelling content and build strong connections with their audience. Technology is not just a tool; it's a catalyst for creativity and innovation in the world of content creation.

Understanding Your Audience

The true essence of success lies in the ability to build meaningful connections with your audience. It's about forging a profound understanding of who your viewers are, what resonates with them, and what they expect from your content.

Before you can establish a connection, you must first understand your audience on a deeper level. It's not merely about the demographics or analytics; it's about grasping the unique personas that make up your viewer base. Who are they? What motivates them? What are their interests and pain points? By delving into these aspects, you can tailor your content to cater to their specific needs and desires.

Engagement is the cornerstone of building connections on YouTube. It's not a one-way communication, but a vibrant, two-way street where creators and viewers engage in a meaningful dialogue. This section explores various avenues for interaction, from responding to comments and messages to conducting live Q&A sessions and polls during live streams. By actively participating in these conversations, you not only strengthen your bond with your audience but also gain valuable insights into their thoughts and preferences.

The art of community building on YouTube revolves around creating an environment where your audience feels a deep sense of belonging and connection to your content and channel. This is achieved through a combination of strategies and actions that foster a strong and loyal community of viewers. Here's an explanation of how to foster this sense of belonging:

Authenticity and Relatability: Being authentic and relatable is crucial. Viewers appreciate creators who are genuine and transparent about their thoughts, experiences, and emotions. Share your personal stories, struggles, and successes to create a more authentic connection with your audience.

Active Engagement: Engaging with your audience actively is a key aspect. Respond to comments on your videos, answer questions, and acknowledge viewers who show support. This interaction not only shows that you value your audience but also makes viewers feel heard and appreciated.

Regular Communication: Keep your audience informed and engaged through regular communication. Share updates about your channel, upcoming content, and personal life through social media, community posts, or video announcements. Consistent communication helps maintain a connection between uploads.

Live Interactions: Hosting live Q&A sessions, live streaming, or interactive events can be powerful ways to engage with your audience in real-time. Live interactions allow viewers to ask questions, share their thoughts, and feel like they're part of a live conversation with you.

Community Contributions: Encourage your audience to contribute to your content. This could include asking for video ideas, fan art, or feedback. By involving your viewers in the creative process, you create a sense of ownership and collaboration within your community.

Shared Values and Interests: Build your community around shared values and interests. If your content aligns with your viewers' passions or beliefs, they are more likely to feel a sense of belonging. This involves understanding your target audience and creating content that resonates with their values.

Consistency: Consistency is key in community building. Maintain a regular upload schedule so that viewers know when to expect new content. Reliability creates a sense of trust, and viewers are more likely to stay engaged if they can rely on your consistent presence.

Moderation and Safety: Ensure that your community is a safe and respectful space for all viewers. Implement moderation tools to handle inappropriate comments or behavior. A positive and welcoming environment encourages viewers to actively participate and engage.

Acknowledgment and Appreciation: Show appreciation for your community's support. Celebrate milestones, such as reaching subscriber goals or video view milestones. Recognizing your audience's role in your success makes them feel valued.

Listening and Adapting: Pay attention to feedback and suggestions from your community. Use their input to shape your content, making them feel like their opinions matter. When viewers see that their feedback leads to positive changes, they become more invested in your channel.

By consistently applying these strategies, YouTubers can foster a sense of belonging among their audience. Building a strong and engaged community not only enhances viewer loyalty but also contributes to the long-term success of a YouTube channel.

Leveraging Analytics for Audience Insights

Mastering the art of harnessing analytics has become paramount. Content creators on platforms like YouTube are continually seeking ways to enhance their viewers' experience, and one of the most potent tools in their arsenal is YouTube analytics. This chapter delves deep into the realm of leveraging analytics to glean invaluable insights into audience preferences and behaviors. It's not just about collecting data; it's about interpreting it effectively to shape your content strategy, drive engagement, and satisfy your viewers.

The YouTube Analytics Toolbox: Your Window into Viewer Behavior

Before we embark on this journey into the world of analytics, it's essential to familiarize ourselves with the YouTube Analytics toolbox. This toolbox, a repository of metrics and data, serves as a window into the behavior of your audience. Each metric is a piece of the puzzle, revealing insights about how viewers interact with your content. It's not merely about the numbers; it's about deciphering what these numbers convey about your audience's preferences and actions.

Understanding Watch Time: The Currency of Engagement

Watch time is the lifeblood of any successful YouTube channel. It is the total number of minutes that viewers have spent watching your videos. However, watch time is not just a metric; it's a reflection of your content's ability to captivate and retain viewers' attention. To harness the power of watch time, creators must delve deep into their analytics to understand trends and identify patterns.

Analyzing watch time data involves examining which videos garnered the most watch time, when viewers tend to watch your content, and how the length of your videos affects watch time. By comprehending these aspects, content creators can make informed decisions about the types of content to produce, the best times to upload, and the ideal video duration.

Moreover, creators can discover content that performs exceptionally well in terms of watch time and attempt to replicate its elements in future videos. This iterative approach, guided by watch time insights, allows creators to fine-tune their content and keep their audience engaged for more extended periods.

Identifying Drop-off Points: Navigating Viewer Retention

Viewer retention is a critical aspect of audience satisfaction. It's not enough to attract viewers; you must also retain their attention throughout your videos. Understanding drop-off points, the moments when viewers tend to lose interest or click away from your content, is pivotal in achieving this.

YouTube analytics provides data on viewer retention, enabling creators to identify precisely when and where viewers tend to drop off. This information empowers creators to tailor their content to maintain engagement throughout the video. Strategies for reducing drop-off points encompass various elements, such as improving pacing, enhancing storytelling, and refining content structure.

By addressing drop-off points, creators can create more compelling and immersive content that holds the viewer's attention from start to finish. Viewer retention isn't just about keeping viewers engaged; it's about delivering a satisfying and immersive viewing experience that keeps them coming back for more.

Click-Through Rates (CTR): The Gateway to Engagement

The gateway to viewer engagement is often found in click-through rates (CTR). CTR measures the effectiveness of your video's title and thumbnail in compelling viewers to click on it. A high CTR indicates that your title and thumbnail successfully enticed viewers to watch your video.

Understanding CTR data involves analyzing how well your titles and thumbnails perform across different videos. Creators can uncover insights into which titles and thumbnails resonate most with their audience. Furthermore, CTR can provide valuable feedback on the effectiveness of A/B testing when experimenting with different titles and thumbnails.

Strategies for optimizing CTR include crafting attention-grabbing titles and thumbnails that not only accurately represent your content but also pique viewers' curiosity. Creators can experiment with various approaches, such as using intriguing visuals or posing compelling questions in their thumbnails.

Armed with insights from YouTube analytics, creators can embark on the journey of tailoring their content to align with what their audience enjoys the most. This data-driven approach encompasses various aspects of content creation, including video topics, formats, and presentation styles.

Understanding what topics resonate with your audience involves analyzing which video topics have garnered the most views, watch time, and engagement. Creators can use this information to prioritize content that aligns with viewer preferences while still allowing room for creative exploration.

Additionally, analytics can shed light on the most effective presentation styles and formats for your audience. Creators can identify whether scripted videos or spontaneous content performs better, and whether viewers prefer longer, in-depth videos or shorter, concise ones.

By aligning content with viewer preferences, creators can foster deeper engagement and deliver content that resonates, resulting in higher viewer satisfaction and loyalty.

Creating Resonant and Engaging Content

Creating content that resonates and engages on YouTube is an intricate and nuanced art. It involves understanding and aligning with your audience's interests, utilizing captivating presentation techniques, balancing innovation with viewer preferences, mastering the art of storytelling, and forging emotional connections.

Deeply understanding viewer interests is fundamental to creating content that resonates. This requires not only identifying topics that captivate your audience but also aligning your content with their desires. The process involves extensive research into viewer preferences, enabling you to craft content that speaks directly to their passions and curiosities.

Engagement is the lifeblood of successful YouTube content. This aspect involves employing a range of presentation techniques to captivate your audience. These techniques include the use of compelling visuals, effective storytelling, strategic humor, and interactive elements. Key to maintaining engagement is the mastery of pacing, timing, and the use of effective transitions, all of which contribute to holding the audience's attention throughout the video.

Balancing innovation with viewer preferences is a delicate act. It involves navigating the fine line between introducing fresh, creative content and remaining within the realms of what your audience appreciates and expects. This balance allows for experimentation with new formats, ideas, and styles, ensuring that content evolves without alienating the existing audience.

The power of storytelling in content creation cannot be overstated. This chapter explores how to weave narratives that resonate emotionally with viewers, incorporating elements like relatable characters, engaging plot arcs, and meaningful themes. Effective storytelling techniques can leave a lasting impression on your audience, deepening their connection with your content.

Forging an emotional connection is essential in transforming your content from mere videos into memorable experiences. This involves infusing your content with authenticity, vulnerability, and relatability, allowing viewers to see reflections of themselves in your narratives. Content that evokes emotions has the power to leave an indelible mark on viewers' hearts.

Creating resonant and engaging content on YouTube is a multifaceted endeavor. It demands a deep understanding of viewer interests, the use of engaging presentation techniques, a balance between innovation and viewer preferences, the artful use of storytelling, and the creation of emotional connections. When these elements are skillfully combined, they transform your content into an experience that resonates profoundly with your audience, leaving a lasting imprint on the digital canvas of YouTube.

Adapting to Changing Audience Preferences

In an environment as fast-paced and ever-changing as YouTube, the ability to evolve and adapt content strategies in response to these changes is crucial for ensuring sustained engagement and relevance.

The first aspect of adaptability involves recognizing and understanding the fluid nature of audience preferences. As cultural trends shift, technological advancements emerge, and societal norms evolve, so too do the interests and preferences of viewers. This fluidity requires content creators to be perpetually vigilant, monitoring changes in viewer behavior and preferences. Utilizing tools such as YouTube analytics, creators can track viewer engagement metrics, understand the demographics of their audience, and identify emerging trends in real-time.

But adaptability goes beyond mere observation; it requires action. This means evolving content strategies to align with these changes. For instance, if analytics reveal a growing interest in a particular topic or format among the audience, content creators might consider incorporating these elements into their videos. This evolution might involve experimenting with new video formats, exploring different content topics, or even adjusting the tone and style of the content to better resonate with the audience's shifting preferences.

Another key element of adaptability is engaging directly with the audience to understand their evolving needs and preferences. This can be achieved through various means such as reading and responding to comments, conducting surveys, or engaging with viewers on social media platforms. Such direct engagement not only provides valuable insights into what the audience enjoys but also helps in building a community around the content, further enhancing viewer loyalty and engagement.

Adapting content strategies also means being mindful of the broader demographic shifts that might be occurring within the audience. For example, if a content creator notices an increasing number of viewers from a different age group or geographical region, it might be beneficial to tailor some aspects of the content to appeal to these new audience segments. This approach ensures that the content remains relevant and appealing to a diverse and evolving viewer base.

Consistency and Persistence

In becoming a successful YouTube influencer, consistency and persistence are key determinants of success. This chapter delves into the importance of these qualities, exploring how they shape the growth of a YouTube channel and the creator's personal brand. It also addresses the challenges faced in maintaining consistency and the resilience required to overcome the inevitable obstacles in a content creator's path.

Consistent Posting Schedule

The importance of a consistent posting schedule on YouTube cannot be overstated. It plays a fundamental role in the success and growth of a YouTube channel. Here's an explanation of why having a consistent posting schedule is crucial:

Audience Expectations: Viewers come to expect and rely on a consistent schedule. When you establish a regular posting routine, your audience knows when to anticipate new content. This predictability encourages viewers to return to your channel at specific times, increasing your video's initial engagement.

Building Trust: Consistency builds trust with your audience. When you consistently deliver content as promised, it demonstrates your reliability as a content creator. Viewers are more likely to trust and invest their time in channels they know will consistently provide valuable content.

Subscriber Retention: A consistent posting schedule helps retain subscribers. Viewers are more likely to subscribe and stay subscribed when they know they can count on a steady stream of content. Inconsistency may lead to subscribers losing interest and unsubscribing.

Audience Growth: YouTube's algorithm rewards channels with consistent posting schedules. Channels that upload content regularly are more likely to be recommended to viewers, leading to increased visibility and potential new subscribers. Consistency can help your channel grow faster.

Improved Engagement: Regular posting keeps your audience engaged. When viewers know when to expect your content, they are more likely to actively participate in discussions, like, comment, and share your videos. This engagement can boost your video's performance and visibility on YouTube.

Content Planning: A consistent schedule forces you to plan your content in advance. This planning can lead to better, more organized content that aligns with your channel's niche and audience preferences. It also allows you to explore creative ideas and themes more effectively.

Time Management: Having a schedule helps content creators manage their time more efficiently. It prevents last-minute rushes and ensures that you have ample time for video production, editing, and promotion. This leads to higher-quality content.

Professionalism: Consistency gives your channel a professional image. It shows that you take your content creation seriously and are committed to providing value to your audience. A well-managed schedule reflects positively on your brand.

SEO Benefits: Consistent posting can improve your channel's search engine optimization (SEO). Regular uploads signal to YouTube's algorithm that your channel is active and relevant, potentially leading to higher search rankings and more discoverability.

Brand Identity: A consistent schedule is a part of your channel's brand identity. It distinguishes your channel from others and reinforces your unique style and content. This consistency can help you stand out in a crowded YouTube landscape.

Maintaining a consistent posting schedule on YouTube is crucial for audience retention, growth, and trust-building. It not only benefits your channel's performance but also enhances your overall content creation experience. As a YouTuber, committing to a consistent posting schedule is a strategic move that can contribute significantly to your channel's success.

Overcoming Challenges and Avoiding Burnout

Burnout among content creators is a prevalent issue in the digital landscape, often stemming from a variety of factors such as creative blocks, the constant pressure to perform, and the overall demanding nature of content creation. This article aims to explore these common reasons for burnout and provide effective strategies for managing and preventing it.

Creative blocks are one of the primary challenges faced by content creators. This can range from writer's block in scripting to a lack of ideas for new videos or content formats. These blocks can be particularly demoralizing as they directly impact a creator's ability to produce new content. Overcoming these blocks involves a combination of tactics, such as taking breaks, seeking inspiration from different sources, and experimenting with new content ideas that can reignite the creative spark.

Content creators often face immense pressure to consistently perform at their best. This pressure can come from the expectations of an ever-growing audience, the creator's personal aspirations, or the standards set by peers and competitors in the field. It's crucial for creators to set realistic goals and understand that not every piece of content will be a viral hit. Balancing ambition with practicality and focusing on gradual growth can help alleviate this pressure.

Content creation, contrary to popular belief, is not always glamorous. It involves a lot of behind-the-scenes work: scripting, filming, editing, marketing, and engaging with the audience. This workload can quickly become overwhelming, especially for solo creators or small teams.

Effective time management, delegating tasks when possible, and utilizing tools to streamline the content creation process can significantly reduce this burden.

Setting Realistic Goals: Creators should set achievable goals and benchmarks for their content and growth. This helps in maintaining a sense of accomplishment and progress without the unrealistic pressure of overnight success.

Diversifying Content Types: Experimenting with different types of content can keep the creative process fresh and exciting. Trying new formats, collaborating with other creators, or venturing into new topics can provide a much-needed change of pace and inspiration.

Maintaining a Healthy Work-Life Balance: It's essential for creators to not let their work consume their entire lives. Setting clear boundaries between work and personal time, engaging in hobbies and activities outside of content creation, and ensuring adequate rest and relaxation are key to maintaining overall well-being and creativity.

Persistence in the Face of Setbacks

In the ever-evolving realm of content creation, particularly on platforms like YouTube, persistence emerges as a linchpin for success. This section delves into why this trait proves invaluable in navigating the tumultuous journey of a content creator, especially when confronting setbacks like variable viewer engagement, unpredictable algorithm changes, or personal challenges.

Content creation is intrinsically tied to fluctuations. Viewer engagement can vary widely, often without clear reasons. The YouTube algorithm, a mysterious and ever-changing beast, can alter content visibility overnight. Additionally, personal challenges, ranging from creative blocks to life circumstances, can impede progress. In this unpredictable environment, persistence is not just a virtue; it's a necessity.

Persistence is the quiet force that enables creators to withstand and thrive amidst these challenges. It's about maintaining focus on long-term goals, even when short-term indicators seem discouraging. This unwavering commitment is what differentiates successful creators from the rest. It's a testament to the belief in one's vision and the resilience to see it through.

Strategies for Cultivating and Maintaining Persistence

Embracing a Growth Mindset: Viewing challenges as opportunities for growth rather than insurmountable obstacles is crucial. This mindset fosters resilience and a willingness to learn from every setback.

Setting Realistic and Incremental Goals: Break down your larger vision into smaller, achievable goals. This strategy allows for a sense of progress and accomplishment, fueling motivation even when the bigger picture seems daunting.

Learning from Failures: Every setback is a lesson in disguise. Analyze what went wrong, adjust your strategies, and move forward with this newfound knowledge. Remember, in the world of content creation, what doesn't work is often as valuable as what does.

Seeking Inspiration and Support: Surround yourself with a network of fellow creators and mentors. This community can offer practical advice, emotional support, and a wellspring of inspiration to keep you moving forward.

Balancing Persistence with Self-Care: Persistence should not come at the cost of personal well-being. It's vital to recognize when to push through and when to take a step back for self-care. Burnout is the antithesis of persistence.

Celebrating Small Victories: Acknowledge and celebrate your achievements, no matter how small. These moments of joy and pride are fuel for the long journey ahead.

Staying Adaptable: The ability to adapt to changes, whether in audience preferences or platform algorithms, is a key component of persistence. Stay informed, be flexible, and be ready to pivot your strategies as needed.

In the end, persistence is more than just a quality; it's the cornerstone of a content creator's journey, turning aspirations into achievements and dreams into realities.

A Marathon, Not a Sprint

In the fast-paced world of digital content, there's a profound truth often overshadowed by the allure of viral hits and overnight sensations: building a successful YouTube channel is a marathon, not a sprint. This post aims to underscore the importance of a long-term vision and the practice of patience in the pursuit of growth and results.

Set Realistic Expectations: It's crucial to understand that growth on YouTube often takes time and may not happen as quickly as one hopes. It's easy to get discouraged when comparing your channel's progress to others, especially those who seem to have achieved success overnight. However, it's important to remember that each channel's journey is unique. Set achievable goals for your channel, whether it's gaining a certain number of subscribers in a month, improving your video editing skills, or simply creating content consistently. Celebrate every milestone, no matter how small - be it your first 100 subscribers or the first time a video hits 1,000 views. These achievements are stepping stones towards your larger goal and should be acknowledged as signs of progress.

Focus on Learning and Improvement: Each video you create and upload is a learning opportunity. Take the time to review audience feedback in the comments, study the analytics provided by YouTube to understand what works and what doesn't. For instance, look at watch time statistics to see where viewers tend to drop off, and adjust your content accordingly. Be open to constructive criticism and willing to adapt. Perhaps try a new editing technique or a different approach to scripting. The key is to continually refine your craft based on direct and indirect feedback, always aiming to improve the quality of your content.

Be Consistent: Consistency is a key factor in building and maintaining an audience. This doesn't necessarily mean posting new content daily, but rather adhering to a regular and predictable schedule that your audience can rely on. Whether it's once a week or twice a month, choose a frequency that you can comfortably maintain. Consistency also applies to the quality of your content. Ensure that each video you post meets a standard of quality that your audience has come to expect from you. This reliability in both schedule and quality helps foster a loyal viewership.

Stay True to Your Passion: In the pursuit of views and subscribers, it's easy to lose sight of why you started creating content in the first place. Staying true to your interests and passions is crucial. Authentic content resonates more deeply with audiences. When you create content you are passionate about, it shows in your work, making it more engaging and relatable. This authenticity also helps in sustaining your motivation over time, as you are more likely to enjoy the content creation process.

Network and Collaborate: Networking with fellow content creators can open doors to new opportunities and insights. Collaborations can introduce your channel to new audiences and add variety to your content. Beyond collaborations, networking can also provide moral support and a sense of community. Engaging with creators who share similar struggles and goals can be incredibly motivating. Attend meetups, join creator forums, and participate in online communities. These connections can offer valuable advice, different perspectives, and innovative ideas.

Adapt and Innovate: The digital landscape, particularly platforms like YouTube, is constantly evolving. Algorithms change, viewer preferences shift, and new trends emerge. Staying adaptable and open to experimentation is key. This might mean trying out new content formats, leveraging emerging trends, or utilizing new YouTube features. Pay attention to the broader shifts in the digital content world and be willing to pivot or tweak your approach accordingly. Flexibility and a willingness to innovate can help in keeping your channel relevant and engaging over time.

Building a successful YouTube channel is a journey marked by persistence, patience, and consistent effort. It's about playing the long game, staying committed to your vision, and understanding that every step, no matter how small, is a step towards achieving your goals. Remember, in the marathon of YouTube, it's not just about how fast you run, but how long you can keep running.

Branding and Marketing

In the world of YouTube, where millions of creators vie for attention, having a distinct and memorable brand is as crucial as the content itself. This chapter draws upon the branding and marketing strategies employed by successful YouTubers like MrBeast and others, offering valuable insights for aspiring influencers.

Your brand is more than just a logo or a color scheme; it's the entire identity of your channel. It encompasses your content style, communication tone, and the values you represent. Successful YouTubers like MrBeast have mastered this, creating a brand that resonates deeply with their audience. Start by asking yourself what you want your channel to be known for. Is it humor, educational content, tech reviews, or lifestyle vlogging? This core identity should be the foundation of all your branding efforts.

Consistency is key in branding. Your channel's visual elements — logo, banner, thumbnails — and tone of voice should be consistent across YouTube and other social media platforms. This uniformity helps in creating a recognizable and professional image. Analyze how successful YouTubers maintain a coherent look and feel across their digital presence, and apply these principles to your brand.

Your channel's visuals are the first thing potential subscribers notice. Invest time in creating an engaging and professional-looking channel art, thumbnail, and logo. Notice how creators like MrBeast use visually compelling thumbnails that are both consistent in style and enticing enough to click. These visuals should reflect your brand's personality and content.

Great branding often involves storytelling. Your personal story, how you started, and what drives you can be powerful elements of your brand. Successful YouTubers often share their journeys, making their channels more relatable and inspiring. Incorporate your personality into your videos; audiences tend to connect more with the person behind the content than the content itself.

Building a community is a crucial aspect of branding. Engage with your audience through comments, social media, and possibly even meetups or live streams. Successful YouTubers often create a sense of belonging among their viewers, turning them into loyal fans. This engagement also provides valuable feedback for refining your brand and content.

Collaborating with other YouTubers and brands can be an effective way to expand your reach and add credibility to your brand. Partnerships should align with your brand's values and content style. Look at how YouTubers like MrBeast collaborate strategically, often boosting their brand visibility and appeal.

Your content strategy should align with your branding goals. Create content that speaks to your target audience and reinforces your brand identity. Additionally, use other marketing tools like SEO optimization for your video titles, descriptions, and tags to increase visibility. Observe how top YouTubers use keywords and trends to their advantage.

Finally, be open to evolving your brand. The digital landscape is constantly changing, and so are audience preferences. Successful YouTubers adapt their branding to stay relevant and fresh. Regularly review your branding strategy and be willing to make changes if necessary.

Building a successful brand on YouTube requires a mix of consistent branding, engaging content, community building, and strategic collaborations. Take inspiration from successful YouTubers, but also carve out your unique identity. With the right branding and marketing strategies, aspiring YouTube influencers can create a lasting and impactful presence in the digital world.

Innovation: The Heartbeat of Success

YouTube, at its core, is a platform driven by creativity and innovation. Viewers flock to YouTube not just for entertainment but for fresh, unique content that stands out in a sea of mediocrity. Successful YouTubers understand this. They push boundaries, experiment with new content formats, and aren't afraid to take risks. MrBeast, for example, is known for his out-of-the-box challenges and philanthropic endeavors, setting him apart from the typical content seen on the platform.

Innovation also means staying ahead of technological advancements and platform updates. Embracing new features like YouTube Shorts, live streaming, or VR content can open up new avenues for creativity and audience engagement.

The most influential YouTubers are often trendsetters. They don't just follow popular trends, they create them. This requires a deep understanding of the audience's evolving tastes and a keen eye for what's next. It's about being proactive, not reactive. This could mean tapping into new niches, starting unique challenges, or even sparking social movements.

Take, for example, the rise of educational content on YouTube. Creators like Vsauce began delving into complex topics in an engaging way, setting a trend for educational content that is both informative and entertaining.

A key component of being an innovator and trendsetter is understanding your audience. This means not just looking at the analytics but engaging with your viewers, soliciting their feedback, and understanding their preferences. Successful YouTubers often adapt their content based on this feedback, ensuring that they stay relevant to their audience's interests while also leading them into new and exciting territories.

The digital landscape is in constant flux, and adaptability is key. What works today might not work tomorrow. Successful YouTubers are flexible and quick to adapt to changing dynamics, whether it's algorithm changes, shifting viewer preferences, or emerging platforms. They're always learning, always evolving, and never resting on their laurels.

Collaborations can be a powerful tool for innovation and trendsetting. By collaborating with other creators, influencers can blend styles, ideas, and audiences to create something truly unique. Collaborations also provide a platform for brainstorming and creative exchange, often leading to groundbreaking content ideas.

Monetization Strategies

For many aspiring content creators, YouTube offers not just a platform for creative expression but also a potential avenue for financial success. However, achieving this success extends far beyond simply creating engaging content; it hinges on strategic monetization. In this section, we explore the various revenue streams leveraged by successful YouTube influencers like MrBeast, offering insights into how to diversify income and effectively utilize the YouTube platform for financial gain.

1. Ad Revenue: The Traditional Path

The most well-known form of YouTube monetization is ad revenue generated through the YouTube Partner Program. Once a channel meets the eligibility requirements (currently 1,000 subscribers and 4,000 watch hours), it can start earning money from ads displayed on its videos. The key here is to create content that not only attracts viewers but is also advertiser-friendly, thus maximizing potential ad revenue.

2. Sponsorships and Brand Deals: Lucrative Partnerships

Sponsorships and brand deals can be significantly more lucrative than traditional ad revenue. Influencers like MrBeast often partner with brands to create sponsored content, where they promote a product or service directly in their videos. To attract such deals, it's essential to build a strong, engaged audience and maintain a professional online presence.

3. Merchandising: Brand Extension

Selling branded merchandise is another effective way to monetize a YouTube channel. This can include anything from T-shirts and hats to more unique items that resonate with your brand and audience. Merchandising not only provides an additional revenue stream but also strengthens your brand presence and deepens the connection with your audience.

4. Fan Funding: Direct Support from Viewers

Platforms like Patreon, along with YouTube's Super Chat and Channel Memberships, enable fans to directly support their favorite creators through monthly payments or one-time donations. This type of funding is particularly beneficial for creators who produce niche content that may not be highly lucrative through ads but has a dedicated fan base.

5. Affiliate Marketing: Earning Commissions

Affiliate marketing involves promoting products and earning a commission for each sale made through your unique referral link. YouTubers often include these links in their video descriptions or pinned comments. This strategy works best when the products are relevant to the content of the channel and the interests of its audience.

6. Courses and Digital Products: Leveraging Expertise

For experts in certain fields, creating and selling online courses or digital products can be a profitable avenue. Whether it's a photography course, a cooking ebook, or a fitness program, leveraging your expertise to create value for your audience can lead to significant earnings.

7. Crowdfunding for Projects

Platforms like Kickstarter or GoFundMe can be used to fund specific projects, like a short film or a new series. This approach is particularly useful for large projects that require upfront investment and is a way to gauge and harness audience interest and support.

8. Diversification: The Key to Stability

Perhaps the most important strategy is diversification. Relying on a single income stream can be risky, as changes to the YouTube algorithm or shifts in viewer behavior can drastically affect earnings. Successful YouTubers like MrBeast diversify their income streams to ensure financial stability and growth.

Monetizing a YouTube channel effectively requires a mix of creativity, strategic planning, and a deep understanding of both your audience and the platform. By exploring and combining these different revenue streams, YouTubers can build a sustainable financial model, turning their passion for content creation into a profitable venture. Remember, the key to financial success on YouTube lies not just in the content you create but in how you leverage it to generate income.

Long-term Growth and Adaptation

In the dynamic and ever-changing world of YouTube, the creators who achieve lasting success are those who master the art of adaptation and focus on long-term growth. This post delves into the essential strategies and mindsets necessary for YouTubers to not only survive but thrive over time. Drawing inspiration from the approaches of successful influencers like MrBeast, we explore the critical importance of adaptation, forward planning, and continuous learning in the realm of YouTube content creation.

The only constant on YouTube is change. Algorithm updates, shifting viewer preferences, and evolving content trends are just a few examples of the fluidity of the platform. Successful YouTubers understand this and are always ready to adapt their content and strategies accordingly. Adaptation might mean pivoting your content to align with emerging trends, experimenting with new video formats, or even rebranding your channel to stay relevant.

Long-term success on YouTube requires more than just reacting to changes; it demands strategic planning. This involves setting clear, achievable goals and outlining a roadmap to reach them. Whether it's expanding your audience, increasing engagement, or enhancing the quality of your content, having a long-term vision guides your efforts and helps you measure progress.

As your channel grows, so will your audience. Understanding and evolving with your audience is crucial. This can be achieved through regular engagement and feedback, analyzing viewer data, and staying attuned to what content resonates most with your viewers. Successful YouTubers often tailor their content over time to match their audience's evolving interests, ensuring a loyal and engaged viewer base.

The world of digital content is not limited to YouTube alone. Embracing new technologies and platforms can open up additional avenues for growth. This might involve using social media to expand your reach, exploring new content platforms, or utilizing the latest video technologies to enhance your content's quality and appeal.

The most successful YouTubers are perpetual learners. They stay updated on the latest industry trends, learn new skills to enhance their content, and continuously seek ways to improve their channel. This could mean taking courses in video production, attending content creation workshops, or simply learning from other successful creators.

Collaborating with other YouTubers and industry professionals is another strategy for long-term growth. Collaborations can bring fresh ideas, new audiences, and valuable learning opportunities. Networking, whether through social media or industry events, can also provide insights and open doors to new possibilities.

While pursuing growth, it's essential to maintain a balance between pushing your channel forward and not losing sight of what made your content appealing in the first place. Authenticity and passion are key components of successful content; preserving these elements while adapting and growing is crucial.

Future Directions

Predicting the future trajectory of a content creator as dynamic and innovative as MrBeast (Jimmy Donaldson) is no easy task. However, by examining his past achievements, current interests, and industry trends, we can make some educated insights into what the future might hold for his channel, his brand, and the broader landscape of content creation.

MrBeast has made a significant mark through his philanthropic efforts. Given his strong commitment to using his platform for social good, it's highly plausible that he will continue, and possibly even amplify, his charitable endeavors. We can anticipate more ambitious projects and fundraisers, potentially addressing a broader spectrum of social and environmental issues.

MrBeast's entrepreneurial ventures, like "MrBeast Burger" and "Feastables," showcase his business acumen. The future may see him expanding further into the business world, perhaps exploring new realms related to food, gaming, or merchandise. This move could also provide new content avenues and partnerships.

Known for his boundary-pushing content, MrBeast is likely to continue experimenting with new content formats. Emerging technologies like virtual reality (VR), augmented reality (AR), and immersive interactive experiences might play a significant role in his future content strategy, offering viewers novel ways to engage with his brand.

MrBeast's history of collaborations with other YouTubers and celebrities suggests that we can expect more high-profile collaborations in the future. These may extend beyond the YouTube sphere, potentially involving mainstream media and entertainment industries, and could bring a fresh dynamic to his content.

As MrBeast's influence expands globally, his content and initiatives may take on a more international flavor. We might see him tackling global issues through philanthropic projects, challenges, or campaigns, thereby amplifying his impact on a worldwide scale.

MrBeast's dedication to philanthropy has already inspired numerous content creators. His ongoing commitment to charitable work is likely to motivate even more creators to use their platforms for social good, potentially leading to a trend of philanthropy in the content creation community.

The high production quality and creativity in MrBeast's videos have set a new benchmark in YouTube content. Future content creators might feel inspired to invest more in production values and innovative storytelling techniques, striving to match or exceed the standards he has set.

A key aspect of MrBeast's success is his authenticity and genuine interaction with his audience. Future content creators will likely recognize the importance of maintaining authenticity and fostering genuine engagement with their viewers as central to building a successful channel.

MrBeast's approach to content – spanning gaming, philanthropy, and entrepreneurship – illustrates the benefits of content diversification. Upcoming creators may look to diversify their content across multiple niches or platforms to broaden their appeal and strengthen their brand.

MrBeast's initiatives have not only entertained but also raised awareness about significant issues. This trend could encourage a larger movement within the content creator community, where more creators leverage their platforms to promote social causes and drive positive change.

MrBeast's entrepreneurial projects serve as a blueprint for how content creators can extend their influence beyond YouTube. Future creators might explore similar business opportunities that align with their content themes and audience interests.

Collaboration has been a cornerstone of MrBeast's journey. His work with friends and fellow creators highlights the power of teamwork and community in the content creation process. This could encourage future creators to actively seek collaborative opportunities as a strategy for growth and innovation.

The potential future directions for MrBeast's channel and brand are as varied as they are exciting. His influence extends beyond his own content, setting trends and inspiring future content creators. Whether through continued philanthropy, entrepreneurial ventures, innovative content, or global initiatives, MrBeast is poised to remain a significant force in the YouTube community and beyond.

Conclusion

MrBeast's journey from a young content creator known as "MrBeast6000" to a global philanthropic and entrepreneurial sensation is nothing short of remarkable. His story offers several key takeaways for aspiring YouTubers and reflects his profound influence on the digital media and entertainment landscape.

MrBeast's success story underscores the importance of persistence and adaptation in the world of YouTube. He began his journey with experimentation, trying out various video formats and content ideas. This willingness to adapt and explore different niches before finding his unique voice and style played a crucial role in his eventual success.

Innovation and risk-taking have been hallmarks of MrBeast's content. He has consistently pushed the boundaries of what is possible on YouTube, embracing unconventional ideas and challenging the status quo. This fearlessness in trying new formats and ideas has set him apart in a crowded digital landscape.

One of MrBeast's most significant strengths is his authenticity and genuine engagement with his audience. He has built a strong and loyal following by being transparent, relatable, and deeply connected to his viewers. This authentic connection is a valuable lesson for aspiring creators aiming to build lasting relationships with their own audiences.

MrBeast's philanthropic initiatives have left an indelible mark on the digital media landscape. He has demonstrated the power of using one's platform for social good, inspiring a new generation of creators to consider the positive impact they can make on the world. His commitment to philanthropy serves as a beacon of hope and a reminder that online influence can be harnessed for meaningful causes.

Collaboration and community-building have been key to MrBeast's journey. His involvement in groups like the Daily Masterminds and his willingness to collaborate with other creators have opened doors to growth and new opportunities. This sense of camaraderie and support within the creator community is a valuable aspect of his success.

Beyond YouTube, MrBeast's influence has extended into various domains, including business and entrepreneurship. His ventures like "MrBeast Burger" showcase how content creators can expand their brands beyond digital media. His success serves as a testament to the entrepreneurial possibilities that can arise from online fame.

MrBeast's journey is a testament to the transformative power of online influence when used for the greater good. His impact on digital media and entertainment transcends views and subscribers, inspiring countless individuals to use their platforms not only for personal gain but also for creating positive change in society. His legacy will continue to inspire and shape the future of content creation and online philanthropy for years to come.